Sniffy
THE VIRTUAL RAT
Lite Version

Tom Alloway
University of Toronto at Mississauga

Greg Wilson
DID Software

Jeff Graham
University of Toronto at Mississauga

Lester Krames
University of Toronto at Mississauga

Wadsworth
Thomson Learning™

Australia • Canada • Mexico • Singapore • Spain • United Kingdom • United States

Psychology Editor: *Marianne Taflinger*
Media Editor: *Leslie Krongold*
Assistant Editor: *Jennifer Wilkinson*
Editorial Assistant: *Suzanne Wood*
Marketing Manager: *Jenna Opp*
Project Editor: *Rita Jaramillo*
Print Buyer: *Stacey Weinberger*

Permissions Editor: *Robert Kauser*
Production Service: *Scratchgravel Publishing Services*
Cover Designer: *Gary Palmatier*
Cover Image: *Tony Stone Images*
Compositor: *Scratchgravel Publishing Services*
Printer: *Globus Printing Company, Inc.*

**For more information, contact
Wadsworth/Thomson Learning
10 Davis Drive
Belmont, CA 94002-3098
USA
http://www.wadsworth.com**

International Headquarters
Thomson Learning
International Division
290 Harbor Drive, 2nd Floor
Stamford, CT 06902-7477
USA

UK/Europe/Middle East/South Africa
Thomson Learning
Berkshire House
168-173 High Holborn
London WC1V 7AA
United Kingdom

Asia
Thomson Learning
60 Albert Street, #15-01
Albert Complex
Singapore 189969

Canada
Nelson Thomson Learning
1120 Birchmount Road
Toronto, Ontario M1K 5G4
Canada

In memory of Edward Thorndike, Ivan Pavlov, and B. F. Skinner

Contents

**4   Schedules of Reinforcement and
the Partial-Reinforcement Effect** **45**

5   Introduction to Classical Conditioning **61**

Preface: Installing and Running Sniffy Lite

System Requirements

Windows

You need an IBM-compatible computer with a 486, Pentium, or later processor, running Windows 95 or later, with at least 16 MB of RAM. (Because at least 8 MB of RAM must be available to the program, 32 MB of RAM are preferred.) The full installation requires about 12 MB of hard-disk space. Sniffy Tutor and related files occupy about half of that space. To optimize animation and appearance, we recommend that you set your computer to display High Color (16-bit). To set your computer's color depth:

1. Use your left mouse button to open the My Computer window by double-clicking on the icon with that name on your Windows desktop.
2. Open Control Panel.
3. Open Display.
4. Click on the Settings tab at the top of the Display Properties dialogue box.
5. Under Color Palette, select High Color (16 bit).
6. Click the OK command button at the dialogue box.
7. Follow any additional instructions that the Windows operating system gives you at this point. It may suggest or require that you restart your computer.

On some computers, the Sniffy Lite program may appear to pause repeatedly while the hard-disk light flashes on and off. This problem occurs when there is not enough RAM available to run the Sniffy Lite program, and the computer is attempting to use virtual memory. If this happens, you need to optimize your computer's memory usage by reducing the number of colors displayed.

Macintosh

You need an Apple Macintosh or compatible computer with 68040, Power PC 601, or later processor, running Mac OS 7.5 or later. The computer must have at least 16 MB of RAM. (Because at least 8 MB of free RAM must be available to the program, 32 MB of RAM are preferred.) A full installation requires about 14 MB of hard-disk space. Sniffy Tutor and related files occupy about half of that hard-disk space.

Installation

Windows

Use your left mouse button to double-click the installer program called Install Sniffy Lite on your Sniffy Lite CD, and follow the instructions as you progress. The first screen that you will see is shown below.

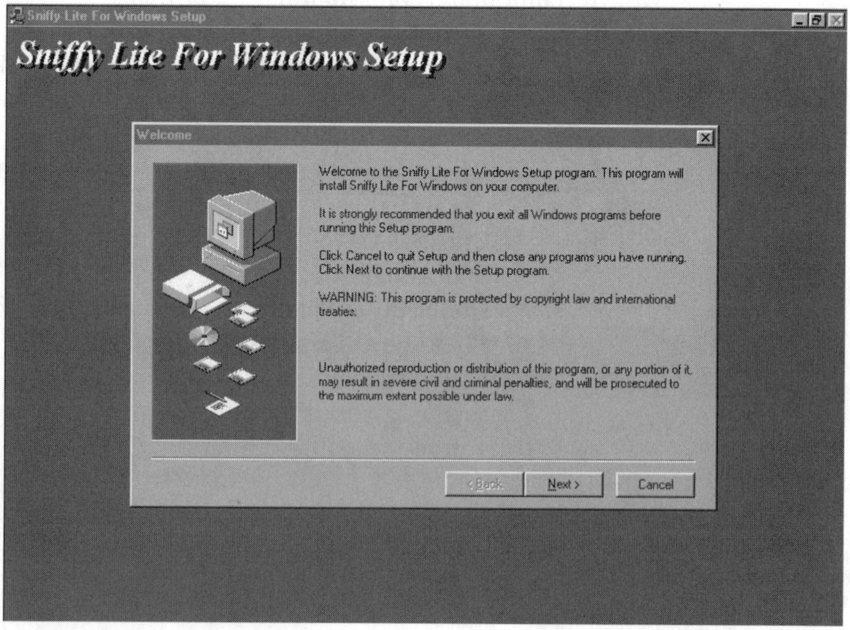

You may choose one of three different installations:

- ■ "Typical" installs the Sniffy Lite program, Sample Files, and Sniffy Tutor.
- ■ "Compact" installs the Sniffy Lite program and Sample Files only.
- ■ "Custom" allows you to choose which components you wish to install. We recommend this option for experienced users only.

Macintosh

Double-clicking the installer program called Install Sniffy Lite will bring up the following screen.

You have three installation options:

- ■ Selecting Easy Install from the pull-down menu before clicking the Install command button will install the Sniffy Lite program, Sample Files, and Sniffy Tutor.
- ■ Selecting Custom Install before clicking Install allows you to select the components you want to install.
- ■ Your third option is to perform a manual installation:
    - □ Expand the CD window and scroll down until you come to the folder called Sniffy Lite for Macintosh.
    - □ Copy this folder to your hard drive.

Starting the Sniffy Lite and Sniffy Tutor Programs

Starting Sniffy Lite

To start the Sniffy Lite program in Windows:

1. The easiest way to start the program is to select Sniffy Lite from the Sniffy Lite for Windows submenu in the Programs section of the Start menu.
2. An alternative way to start the program is to:
   a. Open the Sniffy Lite for Windows folder, which should be located inside the Program Files folder on your C drive.
   b. Use your left mouse button to double-click on the SniffyLite.exe or Sniffy Lite icon. (The .exe extension may or may not be visible, depending on your Windows configuration.)

To start the Sniffy Lite program on a Macintosh:

1. Open the folder called Sniffy Lite for Macintosh. If you installed the program using the installer, this folder will be visible inside your open startup disk window.
2. Double-click the Sniffy Lite program icon.

Starting Sniffy Tutor

Sniffy Tutor offers two 10-minute tours of Sniffy Lite that show you how to set up several of the exercises described in this manual. In Windows, the easiest way to start Sniffy Tutor is by selecting it in the Sniffy Lite for Windows submenu located in the Programs section of the Start menu. On a Macintosh, start Sniffy Tutor by double-clicking the Sniffy Tutor program icon. Sniffy Tutor provides its own self-contained instructions.

 Warning: *If you are trying to run Sniffy Tutor in Windows 95, you may need a file called msvcrt.dll. If you do not have this file, the Windows 95 operating system will tell you that the file is missing when you attempt to run Sniffy Tutor. This problem may arise only with some early versions of Windows 95. This is a well-known Microsoft problem, not a Sniffy software problem. We advise you to talk with our support people at 1-800-423-0563 or to email them at support@kdc.com.*

Contacts, Support, and Information

In the United States:

Wadsworth•Brooks/Cole Publishing Company
10 Davis Drive, Belmont, CA 94002
Call toll free (800) 423-0563 or (800) 354-3706
Fax: (800) 487-8488.
E-mail: sniffy@wadsworth.com

In Canada:

Contact ITP Nelson Canada, College Division, at (800) 668-0671.

For the latest information and updates, check out Sniffy on the Web at:

http://psychology.wadsworth.com/sniffy

To contact the authors via email, write:

Dr. Jeff Graham   jgraham@credit.erin.utoronto.ca
Dr. Tom Alloway   antguy@abspruce.org
Greg Wilson   didsoft@home.com

Acknowledgments

We thank the many students, friends, and colleagues who have helped since the inception of this project in the fall of 1996. Many thanks go to our art director, Allan Sura, and to the high school volunteers who helped with the artwork: Kevin Butler, Tristan Melendreras, Shawn Davis, Rachel Houlton, and Ian Gibb. The research assistants in the Psychology Computer Laboratory were our tireless testers. Special thanks go to our testing team, which included Roc Scalera, Hubert Marczuk, Mike Hynes, Chris England, Anne Dmitrovic, B. J. Balanquit, Kirk Broadhead, and Keith Seim. Allan and Keith were also indispensable in designing and creating the Sniffy Tutor, and B. J. was the webmaster genius who facilitated our continual cross-platform testing. We appreciate the help and support of Professor Doug Chute of Drexel University, who was first "outsider" to see Sniffy's potential and who helped bring it to fruition. We thank the CNN, Télée Quebec, and CBC new teams, who helped promote Sniffy as an ethical alternative to the use of live animals in teaching.

We acknowledge the support of the principal and deans of the University of Toronto at Mississauga, who backed us in the early days before Sniffy attracted the interest of a publisher. We thank the many reviewers who helped refine and polish operational features and pedagogical issues.

Tom Alloway, Jeff Graham, and Lester Krames congratulate our co-author, Greg Wilson, on his achievement in programming Sniffy Lite for the Macintosh and Windows operating systems. Greg tirelessly tackled the complex assignment of converting psychological principles into demonstrable artificial intelligence and did so while dealing with the complex technical problems of cross-platform development.

Finally, we all thank our Wadsworth editorial team, especially Marianne Taflinger and Leslie Krongold.

1

Introduction to Sniffy

Why We Created Sniffy

Sniffy Lite is an affordable and humane way to give college and university students hands-on access to the basic phenomena of operant and classical conditioning that introductory psychology courses and courses on the psychology of learning typically discuss. Although psychologists believe that the phenomena the Sniffy Lite program simulates play a prominent role in both human and animal behavior, courses that discuss these topics are usually taught in a format that gives students no chance to obtain laboratory experience. There are two main reasons for this omission.

The first reason is cost. The most common apparatus that psychologists use to study operant and classical conditioning is the **operant chamber,** a special cage with a lever that a rat can be trained to press and devices for dispensing food and water and presenting other stimuli. A computer connected to the chamber automatically records the rat's responses and controls stimulus presentation. A basic setup consisting of an operant chamber, a computer to control it, and an appropriate interface between the two costs about $3500 in U.S. money. Few schools can afford to purchase this equipment in the quantity required to offer a laboratory component for a course that discusses operant and classical conditioning. In addition, contemporary animal care regulations specify rigorous standards for maintaining animals used for teaching and research. Typically, these regulations not only require that the animals be housed in clean cages and receive adequate food and water, they also specify that animal rooms must receive more fresh air and have better temperature and humidity control than rooms that people occupy. Facilities that comply with these standards are expensive to

build and maintain. To cover these costs, animal facilities usually charge daily maintenance fees for each animal kept, and these fees would add up to a large sum if each student enrolled in the course had his or her own rat to study.

A second reason why students in learning courses rarely have access to animals is that some people think the use of live animals for teaching purposes—where the outcome of each experiment can be confidently predicted on the basis of previous findings—violates the ethical principles of humane animal treatment. Some people hold this view even when the animals used for teaching are never exposed to any discomfort. Opposition is much more widespread if the animals are subjected to noxious stimuli.

Nevertheless, studying animal learning without being able to see how experiments are set up and data are collected isolates students from an important and fascinating set of behavioral phenomena. The Sniffy Lite program is designed to end that isolation.

How We Created Sniffy, the Animated Creature

We created the animated Sniffy character that you see on your computer screen by videotaping a live laboratory rat as it moved around spontaneously in a glass cage with a blue background. The taping sessions occurred in a comfortable, reasonably quiet room, and we just let the rat perform whatever behaviors it happened to produce. From the several hours of videotape that we accumulated, we selected 40 short behavior sequences that show the rat walking around the cage, rearing up against the walls, grooming itself, and performing other typical rat behaviors. Finally, we removed the blue background from each frame of these video clips and adjusted the brightness and contrast in the resulting images to produce almost 600 animation frames that depict the rat in different postures and orientations. The Sniffy Lite program plays these frames in various sequences and positions to produce the virtual animal that you see.

Sniffy, the Program

The Sniffy Lite program lets you set up and perform basic operant and classical conditioning experiments and enables you to collect and dis-

play data in ways that simulate the ways in which psychologists do these things in their laboratories. In addition, because the program both simulates and displays some of the psychological processes that psychologists believe animals (and people) employ, Sniffy Lite shows you some things about learning that you could not observe if you were working with a live animal.

In a real rat, learning is the result of biochemical interactions among billions of neurons in the brain. As a consequence of these physiological processes, animals acquire information about events in the outside world and about how their behavior affects those events. One aspect of learning involves acquiring associations between behaviors (responses) and external events (stimuli), and psychologists call this kind of learning **operant** (or **instrumental**) **conditioning**. A second aspect of learning involves acquiring information about sequences of events in the world. When one stimulus regularly precedes and thus predicts another, animals modify their behavior in certain ways, and psychologists call this kind of learning **classical** (or **respondent**) **conditioning**.

Although we believe that neurophysiological processes in the brain are ultimately responsible for the learned changes in behavior that we observe, psychologists generally discuss operant and classical conditioning in terms of the acquisition and modification of associations. To some extent, we describe learning in associative terms because we do not understand the physiological processes well enough to explain our findings fully in physiological terms. However, psychological and physiological processes also constitute different levels of explanation (Keller & Schoenfeld, 1950; Skinner, 1938). This means we do not need to understand the physiological processes in detail in order to explain learning in psychological terms.

To a degree, the relationship between neurophysiological processes and psychological explanations of learning is analogous to the relationship between the electrical activity in your computer's electronic circuitry and the simulated psychological processes that form the basis for Sniffy's behavior. Your computer contains the equivalent of several million transistors that are in some ways analogous to neurons in a rat's brain. The Sniffy Lite program uses the electronic circuitry of your computer to simulate the psychological mechanisms that many psychologists employ to explain learning in real animals and people. One advantage of computer simulation is that we can program a computer not only to simulate certain psychological processes but also to display those simulations. This fact has enabled us to develop a set of displays that we call **mind windows**. The mind windows show how Sniffy's behavior interacts with the events in the operant chamber to

create, strengthen, and weaken the associations that produce changes in Sniffy's behavior. Thus the Sniffy Lite program not only allows you to set up experiments and record and display behavioral data in a fashion similar to the ways psychologists do these things, it also lets you observe how Sniffy's psychological processes operate. We think that being able to observe Sniffy's psychological processes will make it easier to understand how learning works.

Sniffy Is a Learning Tool, Not a Research Tool

The Sniffy Lite program is the result of developments in computer technology that permit the simulation and display of complex processes on relatively inexpensive personal computers. However, the psychological processes and behavioral phenomena that the program simulates are characteristics of living organisms. Discovering those processes and phenomena required over a century of research with animal and human subjects. Future advances in the scientific understanding of learning will also require research on living organisms. Sniffy Lite and other computer simulations are fascinating tools for demonstrating what we already know, but they cannot substitute for the real thing when it comes to acquiring new scientific insights.

Sniffy is not a real rat. In fact, Sniffy isn't even the most realistic simulation of a real rat that we could have created. The Sniffy Lite program employs a rat as a kind of metaphor to help you understand the psychology of learning. In designing Sniffy as a learning aid, we deliberately sacrificed realism whenever we thought that it got in the way of creating a useful tool for students. For example, you will be using food as a reinforcer (reward) to train Sniffy to press the bar in the operant chamber. Sniffy is always ready to work for food no matter how much he has recently eaten. In contrast, real rats satiate for food and stop working to obtain it when they have had enough. We could have simulated satiation but decided not to because satiation is mainly a motivational, not a learning, phenomenon. If you ever do research using food reinforcement with real animals, you will have to learn how psychologists control for this inconvenient motivational factor when they design learning experiments. However, textbooks on the psychology of learning rarely discuss satiation, psychological explanations of learning phenomena make little reference to it, and we thought that simulating satiation would introduce a needless distraction for students of the psychology of learning.

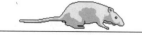

Applying What You Learn from Sniffy

The principles of learning that Sniffy illustrates have many real-world applications in such diverse areas as the therapeutic modification of human behavior and animal training for utility, fun, sport, or profit. In addition to a thorough understanding of learning principles, effectively applying the principles of operant and classical conditioning to real-life situations nearly always involves large measures of creative ingenuity and finesse. To become a practitioner of therapeutic human behavior modification, you need to obtain a bachelor's degree in psychology, attend graduate school, study behavior modification under the direction of a professional, and fulfill the professional licensing requirements of the jurisdiction in which you plan to work. These educational and professional requirements have been established in an effort to ensure the effective and ethical application of the learning principles that Sniffy simulates.

Standards for would-be animal trainers are much less stringent. Anybody can purchase a puppy and attempt to train it. However, if you obtain a puppy and subsequently want to transform the unruly little beast that you actually possess into the obedient, well-behaved member of the household that you had envisioned, you would be well advised to enroll yourself and your puppy in classes at a reputable dog-training school. As is the case with human behavior modification, effective, ethical animal training involves combining a thorough understanding of scientific principles with ingenuity and finesse. The best animal trainers understand both the science and the art. Sniffy will help you learn the science, but you must acquire the art elsewhere. Failure to acquire the art before you try to apply the science can produce unexpected and sometimes even dangerous results.

2 Introduction to Operant Conditioning

Edward Thorndike

The research that led to the study of what today we call operant conditioning began a little over a 100 years ago with the work of Edward Thorndike. Impressed by William James's classic textbook, *Principles of Psychology* (James, 1890), Thorndike enrolled at Harvard University and took courses with James. At Harvard, Thorndike began the first experimental study of learning in animals. At the time, there was no formal psychological laboratory at Harvard and very little money to support Thorndike's work. His first laboratory was in his home.

Thorndike (1898) described his early animal learning experiments in a classic monograph. In these experiments, Thorndike studied the way cats learned to escape from an apparatus that he called a **puzzle box.** The cats were locked inside the box and had to manipulate a mechanical device to open the box and escape. Initially, the cats emitted many different behaviors, most of which did not lead to escape. However, gradually by trial and error, the cats found the behaviors that led to escape. Thorndike recorded how long it took each cat to escape on each trial and found that the average time gradually decreased from several minutes to a few seconds. As the escape speeds increased, the cats were learning to eliminate useless behaviors, while retaining the much smaller number of successful behaviors. The form of learning that Thorndike studied is often called **instrumental conditioning** because the animal's behavior is instrumental in producing certain consequences. Thorndike summarized the mechanism that strengthens

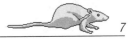

and selects successful behaviors by stating what he called the **law of effect:**

> Of several responses made to the same situation, those which are accompanied or closely followed by satisfaction to the animal will, other things being equal, be more firmly connected with the situation, so that, when it recurs, they will be more likely to recur; those which are accompanied or closely followed by discomfort to the animal will, other things being equal, have their connections with that situation weakened, so that, when it recurs, they will be less likely to occur. The greater the satisfaction or discomfort, the greater the strengthening or weakening of the bond. (quoted by Kimble, 1961, p. 10)

Thorndike's experiments showed that the effect—the consequence—of a behavior determines whether the behavior will be strengthened or weakened. Hitting the right combination of levers in Thorndike's puzzle box had the positive effect of opening the door and letting the cat out of the box. As is the case with most pioneers, Thorndike's models of instrumental conditioning and his statement of the law of effect have been subject to many changes. However, they remain an important cornerstone of our understanding of the learning process.

B. F. Skinner

B. F. Skinner formulated the methods and procedures that describe a variant of Thorndike's instrumental conditioning that Skinner called **operant conditioning.** In Thorndike's work with puzzle boxes and subsequently in his studies of animals learning to run mazes, the learning tasks involved apparatus and procedures in which animals had the opportunity to make a correct response only at certain well-defined times called **trials.** Skinner developed a learning situation in which an animal is confined during training in a cage called an **operant chamber,** which contains a device on which responses can be made as well as a mechanism, called the **magazine,** for the delivery of food. In an operant chamber, animals are trained in an experimental situation in which the opportunity to perform some response is continuously available. Skinner, like Thorndike, was interested in how the consequences of behaviors influence the frequency with which those behaviors are repeated. Skinner's work with operant conditioning is thus an extension of Thorndike's work with instrumental conditioning. Moreover, the

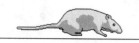

same principles of learning seem to apply both when the animal has the opportunity to make a correct response only at certain times (as in Thorndike's puzzle boxes and mazes) and when the animal is able to respond at any time (as in Skinner's operant chamber).

Skinner (1938) made three fundamental assumptions about behavior:

- Animals are frequently active, which means that organisms are continually **emitting** various behaviors.
- These emitted behaviors frequently have consequences that influence the frequency with which the behaviors are repeated in the future.
- The effects of the consequences are influenced by the animal's motivational state as well as by the physical and social environment. For example, the effect of presenting food as a consequence of performing some behavior will depend on whether the animal has been deprived of food.

Skinner not only studied animal learning, he also believed it was possible to apply his findings to design more effective human institutions in which the planned, systematic application of reinforcement would make people happier and more productive (Skinner, 1953). Skinner not only called for the objective study of behavior, he also posited that behavior is often caused by events in the environment that can be discovered and manipulated to change behavior. In other words, he attempted to create a philosophical framework based on his findings, and this effort generated much excitement and controversy (Skinner, 1971).

Traditionally, people have believed that mental events cause many aspects of human behavior. In contrast, Skinner (1953, 1971) asserted that it is more useful to view feelings, thoughts, emotions, and most other mental events as covert behaviors. In Skinner's view, both overt behaviors and the mental events that accompany them occur because of current and past conditions of reinforcement, and both are subject to the same behavioral laws.

Although he recognized that behavior is produced by the interaction of genetic and environmental factors, Skinner and his followers have concerned themselves almost exclusively with environmental effects. The historical reasons for this emphasis on the environment are complex, but one important reason is that environmental factors are easier to manipulate than genetic factors, especially in human beings, where genetic manipulations are usually considered to be unethical. For example, a child's genes and the environment in which the child grows

up jointly determine how tall the child will grow to be. However, although nothing can be done about a child's tallness genes once the embryo has been conceived, the diet that the child eats—an environmental factor—can significantly affect adult height.

Skinner (1938, 1953) stated that psychologists should be concerned with discovering the laws of behavior and emphasized the importance of relating environmental causes to behavioral effects. In addition, he believed it is often possible to discover behavioral laws without understanding what goes on inside the organism. Many psychologists have employed the metaphor of a black box to characterize this aspect of Skinner's approach to psychology. The box, which represents the organism, is opaque. Not only is the inside invisible, we don't need to know what goes on inside it. Understanding the rules that govern the box's behavior and controlling its actions do not require opening it. In fact, trying to understand what goes on inside the box may be confusing and misleading.

We can understand this "black box" view of the individual by considering the behavior of a television set. Few of us can produce or understand a circuit diagram that explains how a TV set works, but we can still operate one. We know that we must plug the set into an electric outlet. We know that when we manipulate the channel selector, the stations change. We know that a volume control adjusts the loudness, and other controls change the colors. The picture and sound are the behaviors that we want to predict and change, and we can predict and change these behaviors. If the set is not working properly, we also know that sometimes a sharp rap on the side of the case may improve the picture. None of this knowledge about how to change the behavior of a TV set requires understanding its internal workings. Skinner believed we can predict and change the behavior of organisms, including ourselves, in a similar way without needing to understand the internal workings of the body.

Skinner (1938) proposed that psychologists should seek to discover relationships between the environment and behavior without speculating about what goes on inside the organism. However, this "agnostic" approach to the workings of the organism was one of the most controversial aspects of Skinner's approach to psychology. A great many psychologists in Skinner's day (for example, Guthrie, 1960; Hull, 1943, 1952; Tolman, 1932) believed, and a majority of present-day psychologists still maintain, that understanding behavior requires understanding the psychological and/or physiological processes that go on inside the organism. This computer program manual is not the place to debate these profound issues in the philosophy of science. Suffice it to

say that in designing a virtual animal that simulates the behavior of a real rat in an operant chamber, we had to endow Sniffy with certain psychological processes in order to reproduce the results that Skinner and others have obtained. Sniffy's psychological processes are modeled after those discussed in many contemporary textbooks on the psychology of learning (for example, Domjan, 1998; Mazur, 1998; Tarpy, 1997). Nevertheless, there is no way of knowing how closely Sniffy's psychological processes resemble those of real rats. All we can say is that Sniffy's psychological processes, which we display in the various mind windows, illustrate the kinds of processes that many psychologists believe are characteristics of real rats.

Skinner (1935, 1938, 1953) distinguished between elicited and emitted behaviors. An elicited behavior is the specific result of presenting a particular stimulus. Examples of elicited behavior include blowing compressed air into the eye to elicit an eyeblink or placing food on the tongue to elicit salivation. You will study how learning can affect elicited behaviors in experiments on classical conditioning. In contrast, emitted behaviors are responses that occur without any readily identifiable eliciting stimulus. For example, there is no stimulus that will reliably elicit grooming movements or barking from all normal dogs in the same way that placing food on a dog's tongue will elicit salivation.

Many of the behaviors that psychologists are interested in understanding are *emitted*, not *elicited*. Consider the behavior of students during class. Students not only listen to the instructor and take notes, they scratch, yawn, read newspapers, wiggle around in their seats, and exhibit a wealth of other behaviors. Almost all of these behaviors are emitted in the sense that no single stimulus exists whose presentation will reliably elicit any of these behaviors from everyone.

The scientific question to which Skinner sought experimental answers was, What controls the frequency of emitted behaviors? To address this question, Skinner developed the operant chamber, a very simple environment in which he thought it would be possible to discover how the environment determines the frequency with which animals and people produce emitted behaviors.

The Operant Chamber

Sniffy's operant chamber resembles those found in laboratories where psychologists do research on operant conditioning. A look at Sniffy's operant chamber reveals three particularly important objects on the

back wall: a lever, or so-called **bar,** that you will train Sniffy to press, a water spout, and a food hopper. As in all operant conditioning situations, the bar is continuously available for Sniffy to press. The hopper is the device you will use to provide a positive consequence, or **reinforcement,** when Sniffy does something that you want him to do more often. You can program the operant chamber to deliver food pellets automatically when Sniffy presses the bar, or you can dispense pellets manually by hitting the space bar on your computer keyboard or clicking your computer's (left) mouse button while pointing at the bar. Other devices in Sniffy's operant chamber permit you to present other kinds of stimuli. These include a speaker, a light, and the parallel metal bars that form the floor through which electric shocks can be delivered.

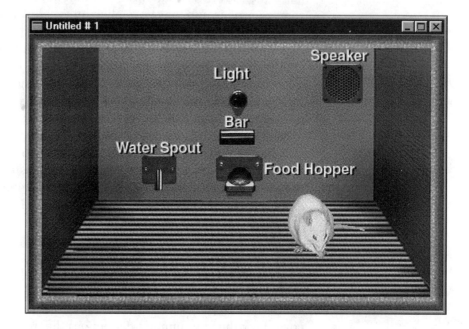

In this restricted environment, a real rat performs a limited subset of species-typical behaviors. As with a real rat, you can expect to see Sniffy rearing up, grooming himself, and exploring the chamber. You can observe and manually record any of the behaviors Sniffy performs. However, the response psychologists generally study in an operant chamber is bar pressing. In research laboratories, psychologists use computers to control the presentation of food and other stimuli and to record bar presses, and the Sniffy Lite program simulates these functions.

Reinforcement and Punishment

Skinner (1938) defined **reinforcement** as a procedure that makes a behavior pattern, or **response,** more likely to be repeated under similar circumstances in the future. In operant conditioning, the term *reinforcement* refers to the procedure of presenting or removing a stimulus (called a **reinforcer**) as a consequence of performing a response. A **positive reinforcer** is a stimulus whose presentation as a consequence of a behavior causes that behavior to occur more frequently under similar circumstances in the future. The term **positive reinforcement** refers to the procedure of presenting a positive reinforcer as a consequence of a behavior pattern. You will use food as a positive reinforcer to train Sniffy to press the bar in the operant chamber. A **negative reinforcer** is a stimulus whose removal or termination as a consequence of a behavior makes that behavior more likely to occur under similar circumstances in the future. The term **negative reinforcement** refers to the procedure of removing a negative reinforcer as a consequence of a behavior. Uncomfortable environmental conditions (temperature extremes, rain) are examples of negative reinforcers, stimuli whose termination can strengthen behaviors. As the old saying goes, most people are smart enough to learn to come in out of the rain. Both positive and negative reinforcement have the effect of increasing the rate (the number of times per minute or hour) at which the reinforced response will occur under similar circumstances in the future.

Skinner (1953, 1971) decried the fact that much of our society is controlled by negative reinforcement. When we have a noisy next-door neighbor, we often bang on the wall to make the noise stop. Termination of the annoyance is negative reinforcement for wall banging under similar circumstances in the future. Children do homework to avoid parental nagging, a woman visits her mother to escape her husband's abusive behavior, a worker shows up for work on time to avoid unemployment. Skinner believed that this heavy reliance on negative reinforcement is a sign of a poorly planned society. He wrote several books and articles describing how society might be better organized based on knowledge of operant principles and extensive use of positive reinforcement.

Operant conditioning also defines two procedures for punishing behavior. **Punishment** is the mirror image of reinforcement. Whereas reinforcement causes behaviors to be repeated more often, punishment causes behaviors to occur less often. A **positive punisher** is a stimulus whose presentation following the occurrence of a response makes that

response occur less often in the future. **Positive punishment** is the name of the procedure involved in presenting a positive punisher as a behavioral consequence. If you hit your puppy with a rolled-up newspaper after it has a toilet accident in the house, you are employing positive punishment. A **negative punisher** is a stimulus whose removal following a response causes that response to occur less often in the future. **Negative punishment** is the procedure involved in removing a negative punisher to make a behavior occur less often. If your daughter misbehaves while watching her favorite television program and you send her to her room (thereby terminating access to the television program), you are employing negative punishment.

Note that the terms *negative* and *positive* have the same meaning when applied to punishment that they have when applied to reinforcement. Both positive reinforcers and positive punishers have their effects respectively of strengthening or weakening behaviors when you apply or turn on the stimuli following a behavior pattern. Both negative reinforcers and negative punishers have their respective effects when the stimuli are removed or terminated. But remember, both positive and negative reinforcement cause behaviors to occur more often, whereas both positive and negative punishment cause behaviors to occur less often.

Another dimension that applies to both reinforcers and punishers concerns whether or not the reinforcing or punishing power of the stimulus is intrinsic or learned. Food is a good example of a stimulus whose reinforcing power is intrinsic in the sense that animals require no special training in order for food to acquire the capacity to act as a positive reinforcer. Similarly, the presentation of electric shock is an intrinsic positive punisher, and the termination of shock is an intrinsic negative reinforcer. Stimuli whose effectiveness as reinforcers or punishers requires no special training are said to be **primary reinforcers** or **punishers.** Other stimuli that lack intrinsic reinforcing or punishing power can acquire the capacity to act as reinforcers or punishers if they are paired with primary reinforcers or punishers. Money is a good example of a stimulus whose reinforcing power has been acquired in this way. There is nothing intrinsically reinforcing about money; it's just pieces of paper and metal disks. However, people learn to treat money as a powerful positive reinforcer because of its pairing with primary reinforcers such as food and drink. Stimuli that acquire reinforcing or punishing power as a result of pairing with primary reinforcers or punishers are called **secondary,** or **conditioned, reinforcers** or **punishers**.

In operant conditioning, subjects learn that particular behaviors produce particular consequences in particular situations. In more techni-

cal terms, many psychologists believe that operant conditioning involves learning a three-part association between a situation, a response, and a reinforcing or punishing consequence (Domjan, 1998; Mazur, 1998; Schwartz & Reisberg, 1991; Tarpy, 1997). The effect of reinforcement is to select for the reinforced behavior at the expense of other unreinforced behaviors. In other words, the effect of reinforcement is to make the reinforced behavior occur more often, and a side effect of reinforcement is that many unreinforced behaviors occur less often, because the subject comes to perform the reinforced behavior so frequently that less time is available to do other things. The effect of punishment is just the opposite of that of reinforcement. Punishment selects against the punished behavior, thereby making it occur less often and, as a side effect, making other unpunished behaviors occur somewhat more often. An animal's **behavioral repertoire** is a list of all the behaviors the animal would ever produce. The effect of operant conditioning is always to modify the relative frequencies of different behaviors in the behavioral repertoire.

Skinner argued that punishment, in either of its forms, is undesirable for several reasons. Apart from ethical considerations, perhaps the most important of these reasons is that punishment is a less effective training tool than reinforcement because punishment conveys less information. When you punish an animal or child for doing something, you are in effect teaching the subject not to perform one particular item in its behavioral repertoire in the situation where the punishment occurred, but punishment provides no information about which other behaviors are appropriate. Reinforcement is a more powerful training tool because reinforcement specifically teaches the organism what to do.

3

Basic Operant Phenomena: Magazine Training, Shaping, Extinction, Spontaneous Recovery, and Secondary Reinforcement

Important Technical Notice

Please read the following very carefully.

❖ The instructions for saving Sniffy Lite files direct you to select an appropriate destination *on your computer's hard disk* for each Sniffy Lite file that you want to save. *It is extremely important that you get into the habit of saving your Sniffy Lite files on the hard disk of the computer that you are using, not on a floppy disk.* Sniffy files can grow quite large. If you try to save a large Sniffy file on a floppy disk that does not have enough room to accommodate it, the program will not be able to save the file successfully. All the time and effort you have invested in doing an exercise may be lost. This potential problem results from the limited storage capacity of floppy disks. It is *not* a problem with the Sniffy Lite program. Similar problems arise with any program that produces large files.

❖ If your instructor wants you to hand in your Sniffy Lite files on floppy disks, initially save the files on your computer's hard disk and then copy the files from the hard disk onto one or more floppy disks.

❖ If you do not have your own computer and must therefore store your Sniffy Lite files on floppy disks, initially save the file on the hard disk of the computer you're using, and then copy the files onto one or more floppy disks. You should then copy the files from the floppy disks back onto the hard disk of the computer you're using before you try to work with the files again.

❖ Keep track of where you save your Sniffy Lite files on your computer's hard disk so you can find them easily.

❖ If you know about the difference between hard disks and floppy disks, about how to select a location for saving files on a hard disk, and about how to copy a file from your hard disk onto a floppy disk or from a floppy disk to a hard disk, consider yourself a reasonably sophisticated computer user. A small pat on the back is in order.

❖ However, if any terms used in this section are unfamiliar to you, or if you are not absolutely certain you know how to do the things described, you need to read the material contained in Appendix 2: How to Manage Your Sniffy Lite Files, which is located at the end of this manual. This appendix contains all the information that you will need to successfully handle your Sniffy Lite files (and the files that you create in any other computer program).

A First Look at Sniffy Lite

The time has come to have a look at the Sniffy Lite program and to begin Sniffy's training.[1]

1. Locate the folder where you installed the Sniffy Lite program and sample files on your computer's hard disk.
2. In Windows, unless you directed the Installer program to do otherwise, it installed Sniffy Lite and associated files in a folder called Sniffy Lite for Windows, which is inside the Program Files folder on your C drive.
3. On a Macintosh, unless you directed the Installer to do something else, it placed the Sniffy Lite program and associated files in a folder called Sniffy Lite for Macintosh, which is at the root level of your startup disk.
4. Start the program.
   a. In Windows, the simplest way is to select the Sniffy Lite program from the Programs section of the Start menu. Another way is to left double-click the program icon inside your Sniffy Lite for Windows folder.
   b. On a Macintosh, the simplest way to start the program is to open your Sniffy Lite for Macintosh folder and double-click the program icon.

[1]In this manual, specific, detailed instructions for performing particular exercises are presented with a gray background.

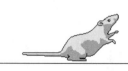

Depending on whether you're running Sniffy Lite under Windows or the Mac OS, when the program opens, your computer screen should look something like one of the following pictures.

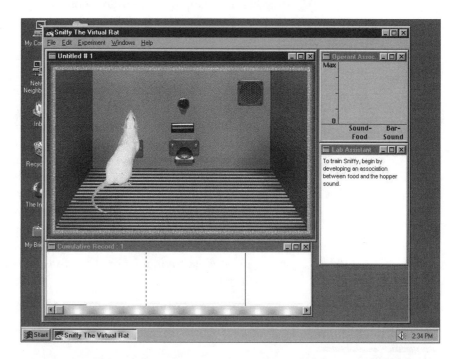

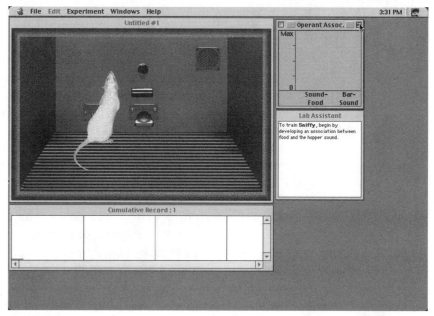

When you first start Sniffy Lite, four windows will be visible:

- In the Operant Chamber window you see Sniffy moving about. The title bar at the top of the window contains the name of the Sniffy file that is currently being run. Because you have not yet saved a Sniffy file, the file is called Untitled.
- In the Operant Associations window you can observe the development of two crucial associations that the Sniffy Lite program's operant conditioning algorithm employs to cause Sniffy to press the bar more often after training than before training. This window is a mind window that shows you two important psychological processes going on inside the Sniffy Lite program. Like all the Sniffy Lite program's mind windows, it has a blue background.
- The Cumulative Record is a window that will enable you to observe changes in Sniffy's bar-pressing rate. Like all the windows in the Sniffy Lite program that provide measures of Sniffy's behavior, the Cumulative Record window has a white background.
- Finally, the Lab Assistant window provides you with useful suggestions about what to do next or about the status of your current Sniffy experiment.

Operant Conditioning: Technique

Like a real rat, Sniffy will occasionally press the bar in the operant chamber even before you train him to do so. Thus, when you condition Sniffy to press the bar, you are not teaching him to do something he was previously incapable of doing. Reinforcement simply increases the frequency with which bar pressing occurs. To train Sniffy to bar-press, you will administer a food pellet for each bar press. Thus you will be using positive reinforcement to train Sniffy.

From what we've said so far, you might think that all you need to do to train Sniffy to bar-press is to set up the operant chamber so that the magazine releases a food pellet each time Sniffy presses the bar. In fact, if that's all you do, Sniffy will eventually learn to press the bar, but he will take a long time to do so. The reason for this slowness illustrates one of the most basic principles of operant conditioning: To be effective, reinforcement must occur *immediately* after the response. Delayed reinforcement is much less effective. The problem with food as a reinforcer in this situation is that, even though a food pellet drops into the food hopper as soon as Sniffy presses the bar, the food can have no effect on Sniffy until he finds it, and Sniffy may not find the food immediately. When he does find it, the food will strengthen whatever behavior Sniffy was performing just before he found it, and that behavior is much more likely to be sniffing around the hopper than bar pressing.

Food is a very effective reinforcer that can be used to train animals to do many kinds of things, but it is often hard to deliver food fast enough to effectively reinforce the response that the trainer wants to strengthen. To overcome this difficulty, animal trainers often transform a stimulus whose timing they can precisely control into a secondary reinforcer by associating that stimulus with food. Then the trainer uses the secondary reinforcer to increase the frequency of the response that the trainer wants the animal to learn. Fortunately, the magazine in an operant chamber produces a distinctive mechanical sound when it drops a food pellet into the hopper; and it is easy to transform this sound, which has no intrinsic power to act as a reinforcer, into a secondary reinforcer by pairing the sound with food delivery in a way that causes Sniffy to associate the sound with food presentation. The procedure that turns the magazine sound into a secondary reinforcer is called **magazine training.**

Exercise 1. Magazine Training

Magazine training is a technique that involves using what amounts to a classical conditioning procedure to turn an originally neutral stimulus into a *secondary reinforcer*. The training process involves an interaction between you and Sniffy. What you will do depends on what Sniffy does, and Sniffy's future responses to the magazine sound will depend on what you do. The idea is to operate the magazine to present pellets of food in such a way that Sniffy learns to associate the sound of the magazine with the availability of a food pellet in the hopper. One association that the Operant Associations mind window displays is the Sound-Food association. By keeping an eye on the Operant Associations mind window, you can watch Sniffy's association between the magazine sound and food develop.

Here are the steps that you need to follow to magazine-train Sniffy:

> 1. If the Sniffy Lite program is not running, start it by double-clicking the program icon. Windows users can also start the program by selecting it from the Programs section of the Start menu.

2. Wait until Sniffy closely approaches the food hopper as he wanders around the operant chamber. Then deliver a food pellet either by pressing the space bar on your computer keyboard or by clicking your (left) mouse button while pointing at the bar.

3. To save time at the start, you may want to give Sniffy several pellets in rapid succession before he wanders away from the hopper.

4. After Sniffy has received several pellets, you can let him wander away a short distance before giving him the next pellet.

5. Keep an eye on the Operant Associations mind window. Sniffy is fully magazine trained when the vertical bar for the Sound-Food association reaches its maximum level. At that point, no matter where Sniffy is in the operant chamber, he will orient toward the hopper and go get the food pellet whenever he hears the sound of the magazine. The following figure depicts what the Operant Associations mind window will look like when Sniffy has been fully magazine-trained. (The figure depicts the appearance of this window in the Windows version of Sniffy Lite. If you are working on a Macintosh, the title bar (top part) of the window will look somewhat different. In this manual, you will see a mixture of Windows- and Macintosh-based illustrations. We based our illustrations on both versions of the program so that neither Windows nor Macintosh users would feel left out.)

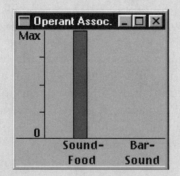

6. When Sniffy has been fully trained, the Lab Assistant will also tell you so and present an abbreviated version of the following instructions about how to train Sniffy to press the bar.

7. When Sniffy has completed magazine training, you should save your magazine-trained Sniffy as a Sniffy Lite program file. To save the file:
   a. Select the Save command from the File menu.
   b. Select an appropriate file name (such as Ex1-MagTrain) and type it into the appropriate space in the Save dialogue box.
   c. Select an appropriate destination for the file on your computer's hard disk. If you need help finding an appropriate place to save your file, read Appendix 2: How to Manage Your Sniffy Lite Files, which contains detailed instructions about the file-saving process and about selecting an appropriate location for your files.
   d. Click the Save command button on the dialogue box.

Exercise 2. Shaping: Teaching Sniffy to Press the Bar

After magazine training, if the operant chamber is programmed to drop a pellet of food into the hopper every time Sniffy presses the bar, Sniffy's occasional spontaneous bar presses will be effectively reinforced; and Sniffy will learn to bar-press all by himself if you just leave him alone. Moreover, he will do so much more quickly than would have been the case without magazine training. However, if you are observant and have a good sense of timing, you can accelerate this learning process by using a technique called **shaping**.

Shaping is the technical name of the procedure employed to train an animal to do something by reinforcing successive approximations of the desired **target behavior**. Shaping is a procedure in which the trainer (teacher) leads the subject (learner) to progress by small steps. Reinforcement is delivered for progress and then withheld until more progress has been made.

To be a successful shaper, you must observe carefully and patiently. Shaping works because behavior is variable. The idea is to pick a behavior that the animal performs fairly often and that is similar in some way to the target behavior you want the animal to perform eventually. Reinforcing this first approximation of the behavior will cause Sniffy to perform that behavior more frequently. Because Sniffy's behavior is composed of movements that occur with different probabilities, you will notice a number of different variations. Eventually Sniffy will

perform a variant of the behavior that resembles the target behavior more closely. That variant then becomes your second approximation, and you require him to repeat that variant to obtain reinforcement. As the second approximation is performed more frequently, Sniffy will eventually emit another variant that resembles the target even more closely, and so on.

Shaping an animal takes patience, careful observation, and good timing. It is a skill you learn with practice. Sniffy is somewhat easier to shape than a real rat partly because he never becomes satiated for food and partly because his behavioral repertoire is smaller than a real rat's. Nevertheless, shaping Sniffy is challenging enough for you to get some idea of both the frustration and the eventual feeling of triumph that shaping an animal engenders.

In the Sniffy Lite program, bar pressing is part of a **response class** (a group of similar movements) in which Sniffy lifts his front paws off the floor of the chamber and places them against a wall. We programmed Sniffy that way because to press the bar, Sniffy must first go to the bar and then rear up in front of it. Thus, as your first approximation to bar pressing, try reinforcing Sniffy for rearing up anywhere in the operant chamber. Once his rearing behavior has become more frequent, require him to rear up against the back wall where the bar is located. Then gradually require him to rear up closer and closer to the bar. If your patience, observational skills, and timing are good, you should have Sniffy bar pressing frequently in 30 minutes or less. If you are very skillful, you can shape Sniffy in less than 10 minutes. However, if you are inattentive or have bad timing, you might have been better off letting Sniffy learn to bar press on his own after magazine training.[2]

Shaping is such an attention-demanding task that you should not pay attention to anything but Sniffy's behavior while you are shaping. However, once Sniffy has pressed the bar four or five times in a minute, you can stop shaping him and watch the progressive effect of reinforcement as Sniffy presses the bar more and more often. At that point, you should start keeping an eye on the Operant Associations mind window in order to observe the development of Sniffy's associa-

---

[2]We suggest that you begin shaping Sniffy by reinforcing him for rearing up against a wall anywhere in the operant chamber. We suggest this approach because in the Sniffy Lite program, bar pressing is part of the wall-rearing response class. Thus, when you reinforce Sniffy for rearing up anywhere in the cage, you increase the probability of all his rearing-up behaviors, including the probability of bar pressing if Sniffy happens to be in front of the bar. Psychologists who study operant conditioning in live rats approach shaping in a variety of ways. Some people start the shaping process by reinforcing the rat whenever it approaches the bar. Others begin by reinforcing the rat whenever it turns toward the bar. Many of these alternative approaches also work well with Sniffy.

tion between pressing the bar and the sound of the magazine. The Operant Associations window displays this as the Bar-Sound association. Sniffy has been completely trained when the vertical column for this association reaches the highest level.

Here is a detailed description of the steps that you should follow to shape Sniffy to press the bar:

1. If the program is not running, start it and use the Open command under the File menu to open the file you saved at the end of magazine training.

2. Select the Save As command from the File menu to give the file an appropriate new name (such as Ex2-acq for acquisition) and save it in the folder where you have decided to keep your Sniffy Lite files on your computer's hard drive. *Saving the file with a new name before you start shaping Sniffy preserves your original magazine-training file for future use.* If your first attempt at shaping is unsuccessful, you can go back and try again without having to magazine-train Sniffy again.

3. (If you were working with a real rat, you would need to make sure the equipment was programmed to deliver a food pellet every time the rat pressed the bar. In the Sniffy Lite program, **continuous reinforcement** (the procedure of reinforcing every instance of the target behavior) is the default condition in effect unless you select some other procedure. Sniffy will receive a food pellet for every bar press unless you have changed the default setting in the Design Operant Experiment dialogue box.)

4. As your first approximation to bar pressing, reinforce Sniffy when he rears up anywhere in the operant chamber.

5. Once rearing has become more common, reinforce Sniffy only when he rears up against the back wall of the operant chamber where the bar is located.

6. Gradually require Sniffy to rear up closer and closer to the bar.

7. Whenever Sniffy rears up directly in front of the bar, there is a chance he will press it. If he does press the bar, he will hear the magazine sound, receive a food pellet, and the Bar-Sound association will start to develop, as evidenced by the appearance of the red column above the words "Bar-Sound" in the Operant Associations mind window. However, the next time that you reinforce Sniffy simply for rearing, the Bar-Sound association column will move down a notch because you have reinforced

Sniffy for doing something other than pressing the bar. Don't worry about the fact that reinforcing rearing causes the Bar-Sound association to weaken or disappear. Continue to reinforce Sniffy for rearing up along the back wall near the bar. Sooner or later he will press the bar again.

8. Each time Sniffy presses the bar, watch closely what he does after eating the food pellet. He might press the bar again a second time either immediately or after rearing up near the bar a time or two. If he does press the bar again, you know you're making progress. Allow him to continue pressing the bar as long as he will do so. However, if he rears up more than twice without pressing the bar again, continue to reinforce rearing up near the bar.

9. If you are patient, the time will come when Sniffy will press the bar four or five times in rapid succession. At that point, you can stop shaping, sit back, and watch the progressive effect of reinforcement as Sniffy continues to press the bar more and more frequently.

10. Watch the rising level of the Bar-Sound association in the Operant Associations mind window. Sniffy's training is complete when that association reaches its maximum level. The following figure depicts what the Operant Associations mind window will look like when Sniffy's training is complete.

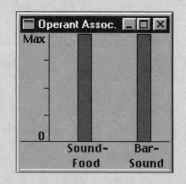

11. When Sniffy is fully trained, select the Save command from the File menu to preserve your trained Sniffy for future use.

Exercise 3. Cumulative Records: Visualizing Sniffy's Bar-Press Performance

In this exercise, you will learn how to interpret **cumulative records,** the means of recording and displaying a rat's bar-pressing behavior that B. F. Skinner (1930) invented. Although there is nothing specific for you to do with Sniffy in this exercise, we suggest you read the following paragraphs while seated in front of your computer with the program running so you can look at Sniffy's cumulative record from time to time to check out the various features we are going to describe.

1. If the Sniffy Lite program is not running, start it.
2. Use the Open command under the File menu to open the file we suggested you name Ex2-acq in Exercise 2.
3. Cumulative Record 1 should be visible under the Operant Chamber window. If it is not visible, you can make it visible by selecting it from the Response Measures section of the Windows menu.
4. Note that as time passes, the visible part of the cumulative record automatically scrolls to the right to follow Sniffy's current behavior. If you want to look at something that happened earlier, you can use the scroll bar at the bottom of the window to scroll back to the left.

How do we know whether a rat has learned anything as a result of training in the operant chamber? With Sniffy, you can observe the learning process directly in the Operant Associations mind window. However, when dealing with real animals whose psychological processes are invisible, psychologists treat learning as a process whose operation they must infer solely on the basis of changes in behavior.

Because bar pressing becomes more frequent as a result of training, Skinner chose to measure learning in the operant chamber as an increase in the frequency of bar pressing. To make the necessary measurements, he invented the **cumulative recorder.** Skinner's cumulative recorder was a mechanical device that pulled a long roll of paper at a constant speed under a pen that rested on the moving paper. At the start, the pen was positioned at the bottom of the record; if the rat did not press the bar, the pen would simply draw a long, straight horizontal line. However, every time the rat pressed the bar, the pen moved a notch upward toward the top of the paper. When the rat was pressing

the bar, the resulting record was a sloping line that moved from the bottom edge toward the top of the record. The more rapidly the rat responded, the steeper the slope of line. In other words, Skinner's cumulative recorder drew a record in which the steepness of the line was directly proportional to the rate of bar pressing.

The roll of paper that Skinner used in his cumulative recorder was not very wide. After recording a certain number of responses, the slanted line would reach the top edge of the paper. When that happened, the pen very quickly reset to the bottom edge of the paper, causing a vertical line to be drawn across the paper from top to bottom. This pattern of a slanted line working its way to the top of the paper followed by a sharp straight line to the bottom of the page gives a cumulative record the appearance of mountain peaks or waves.

These days, mechanical cumulative recorders of the sort that Skinner invented are obsolete. Scientists who study operant conditioning use computers to draw cumulative records of bar pressing in a fashion similar to the way the Sniffy Lite program produces them. We have described the workings of Skinner's original mechanical device because we think that its operation is easier to understand than that of a computer program that simulates it.

There are several important things to remember about the cumulative records that the Sniffy Lite program produces and about cumulative records in general:

- The slope of the rising lines on the graph represents the speed with which Sniffy is pressing the bar. The steeper the slope, the more rapidly Sniffy was pressing when the record was made. If Sniffy is pressing the bar slowly, the slanted line will take a long time to reach the top of the paper where it resets to the bottom. This will result in a record that looks like gentle, undulating waves. If Sniffy is pressing fast, the slanted line will reach the top faster, the pen will have to reset more often, and the resulting record will look like more and steeper "waves."
- Reinforced responses are marked by a short, oblique lines drawn through the record.
- If you let it run long enough, the Sniffy Lite program will produce a series of 10 Cumulative Record windows. The Cumulative Record windows, which are called "Cumulative Record 1," "Cumulative Record 2," and so on, are accessible under the Response Measures section of the Windows menu.
- Each Cumulative Record window depicts Sniffy's bar-pressing performance over a period of approximately two hours of Sniffy Lite

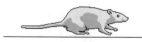

program time. Program time and clock time are not the same thing. The relationship between program time and clock time depends on both the speed of your computer and the animation speed. You can adjust the animation speed in the dialogue box that appears when you execute the Preferences command under the File menu. When the animation speed has been adjusted so that Sniffy is moving at a rate that looks realistic, program time and clock time should pass at approximately the same rates.

- The fact that there is a maximum of 10 Cumulative Record windows means that no Sniffy experiment can last more than about 20 hours in program time. After that program time limit has been reached, you can examine and save your results; but you cannot add any additional stages to that particular Sniffy Lite file.

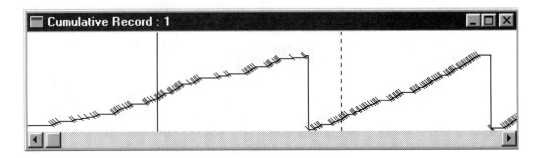

The cumulative record depicted here shows the acquisition of bar pressing as a consequence of shaping in a "typical" experiment. No two cumulative records are ever exactly alike, because Sniffy never behaves in exactly the same way in any two experiments. However, if you were a successful shaper, the part of your cumulative record from Exercise 2 that recorded Sniffy's acquisition of the bar-pressing response should resemble the one just shown. Here are some characteristic things about this record that you can expect to see in your own cumulative record:

- At the far left-hand side, the flat, horizontal line shows that Sniffy has not yet learned to press the bar.
- Sniffy begins to press the bar quite slowly at first and then more and more frequently.
- Note that the steepness of the cumulative record increases rather rapidly at first and then more slowly. In the record just shown, the trend toward an increase in the steepness of the record, which means that Sniffy is pressing faster and faster, continues until a maximum

response rate is reached after the pen resets to the bottom of the record for the first time. A similar increase in the rate of bar pressing should be visible in your record. However, its relationship to pen resets is likely to be different.

■ In addition to depicting Sniffy's response rate and showing which responses were reinforced, the cumulative records that the Sniffy Lite program produces denote the times at which a variety of other significant events occur during experiments. We will explain these additional features in connection with descriptions of experiments where they are important.

Here are a couple of important features that are specific to the cumulative records that the Sniffy Lite program produces:

■ The "height" of Sniffy's cumulative record is always 75 responses. There are always 75 responses between any two consecutive pen resets. When the pen resets the first time, Sniffy has made 75 responses. When it resets the second time, he has made 150 responses, and so on. Knowing this will come in handy later on when you need to figure out how many responses Sniffy has made.

■ In addition to the rather heavy, dark vertical lines that the cumulative record produces when the pen resets from the top of the record to the bottom, there are thinner, alternating solid and dotted vertical lines spaced at regular intervals. These thinner vertical lines are 5-minute time markers. The time between a one thin vertical line and the next (that is, between a solid line and the next dotted line or a dotted line and the next solid line) is 5 minutes in Sniffy Lite program time; and the time between two successive solid or two successive dotted vertical lines is 10 minutes in program time.

Accelerating Time

Even though Sniffy learns some things much faster than a real rat, some of the Sniffy Lite experiments that you will be performing require rather a long time to complete when your computer is displaying all Sniffy's movements. To enable you to run long experiments faster, we have made it possible for you to make Sniffy invisible so that your computer can run the experiments as fast as possible. Selecting the **Isolate Sniffy (Accelerate Time)** command from the Experiment menu encloses Sniffy's operant chamber in a sound-proof, air-conditioned con-

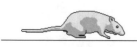

tainer of the type used in many laboratories to isolate an easily distractible live animal from extraneous stimuli that might divert the animal's attention from the experiment itself. The amount of time acceleration that isolating Sniffy will achieve for you depends on the speed of your computer. With a relatively slow computer, 5 minutes of program time may pass in 90 seconds. With a fast computer, 5 minutes of program time may be compressed into 15 seconds or even less. To make Sniffy visible again, choose the **Show Sniffy** command from the Experiment menu. The Isolate Sniffy (Accelerate Time) and Show Sniffy commands replace each other in the Experiment menu. The Isolate Sniffy (Accelerate Time) command is available whenever Sniffy is visible. The Show Sniffy command is available whenever Sniffy is isolated.

 Warning: *If you are running an experiment using time acceleration and want to be able to add new stages to the experiment later, you need to keep an eye on things and stop the experiment when the exercise you are currently performing is complete. For example, if your computer is able to run an experiment 20 times faster than clock time when Sniffy is invisible, an hour of program time will elapse in just 3 minutes, and your computer will run through all 10 cumulative records that the program is capable of producing (that is, it will collect about 20 program hours' worth of data) in about one hour of clock time. For this reason, it's easy to slip up and run an experiment for several "hours" longer than you intended.*

Exercise 4 (Optional). Training Real Animals

Limitations in the Sniffy simulation mean that you cannot train Sniffy to perform completely novel behaviors such as turning somersaults. However, animal trainers routinely use shaping to teach real animals to do things that are physically possible but that an untrained animal might never do. For example, training a physically fit cat to sit up and beg for food and to stand or walk on its hind legs without support is a fairly straightforward process even though untrained cats rarely, if ever, do these things.

Pet food manufacturers produce bite-size cat treats in several flavors, and it is often possible to find a flavor your cat likes so much that the animal will work to obtain them. In fact, the cat may like them so

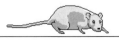

much that you'll have to keep the treats container locked away to prevent theft. Once you've found your cat's favorite, the treats will constitute a primary reinforcer that you can employ to teach the animal to sit up and beg, to stand and walk on its hind legs, or to do other tricks.

As with Sniffy, the first step in training your cat will be magazine training. You need to find a stimulus that can be delivered with split-second timing when your cat does something right and that can be easily transformed into a secondary reinforcer by pairing it with treat presentation. Stores that sell party supplies often stock a variety of noisemakers. You need a small, easy-to-manipulate device that makes a distinctive clicking or popping sound.

You magazine-train your cat in much the same way that you magazine-trained Sniffy. To begin, wait until the cat is near you. Then operate the noisemaker and give the cat a treat. After you have sounded the clicker and given the cat a treat a couple of times with the cat very close by, walk a short distance away before sounding the clicker and giving your cat the next treat. You will know your cat is well magazine-trained when you can call it from anywhere in the house (or neighborhood!) just by sounding the clicker.

Training a cat to sit up and beg or to stand on its hind legs involves requiring the animal to raise its head progressively higher and higher off the ground before you reinforce it by sounding the noisemaker and giving it a treat. Start by watching the cat until it lifts its head somewhat higher than usual. (Standing with its front paws up on something doesn't count.) Then sound the clicker and give the cat a treat. After several reinforcements, the cat will begin walking around with its head held high more often. Because the cat's behavior is variable, sooner or later it will raise its head higher than your first criterion level, and that new higher level then becomes your second approximation that the cat must match to get additional treats. By the time you have reached the third or fourth approximation, the cat will probably be sitting on its hind legs with its front paws off the ground. Once the cat starts to lift its front paws off the ground, it will rather quickly reach a training plateau in which it sits up and "begs" for treats. Depending on your patience, you can either decide that sitting up is good enough or elect to embark on the somewhat more challenging task of shaping the cat to stand on its hind legs and walk.

Once the cat is sitting up, it may or may not spontaneously start to stand on its hind legs. Some cats do, but many don't. If the cat just sits there without starting to rise up on its hind legs, try to elicit standing by holding a treat above the cat's head. Then, as soon as the cat starts

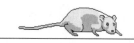

to rise, sound the clicker and give it the treat. On the next trial, wait a bit before again eliciting a stand by holding out a treat. If you are patient enough, the animal will eventually start to stand on its hind legs spontaneously. Finally, if you want the animal to walk on its hind legs, you will have to wait for or elicit behavioral variants in which the animal not only stands up on its hind legs but walks increasingly long distances before you sound the clicker and give it a treat.

If you decide to train your cat, you will discover that training a real animal is somewhat harder than training Sniffy. One reason for the difference is that your cat has a larger behavior repertoire than Sniffy, and another is that the cat is free to move about and approach you in a way that Sniffy cannot. One difficulty will almost certainly arise. During magazine training, when you start to move away from the cat, it will follow you. If you sit down with the treats and clicker in hand, the cat will jump into your lap. If you are standing up and walking, the cat may jump on your shoulder. When these problems arise, don't punish the cat. You will significantly retard the learning process if you do anything to frighten the animal. However, if you never give the cat a treat unless you have first sounded the clicker, and if you never sound the clicker unless the cat is on the floor, the cat will eventually learn to stay off you and "cooperate."

"Clicker training" is also a technique that some dog trainers employ. However, because dogs form stronger social bonds with people than cats do, enthusiastic verbal praise and physical affection are often the only reinforcers that dogs require. For a dog, the verbal praise probably comes to act as a secondary reinforcer that predicts the availability of physical affection. Whether treats should ever be used in addition to physical affection is a somewhat controversial issue among dog trainers.

Another variant of operant conditioning that professional animal trainers use to teach animals to perform sequences of behaviors is called *backward chaining*. For example, suppose you wanted to train a rat to climb a ladder, walk across an elevated plank to a door, and open the door to obtain food. You would first train the rat to go through the open door to the food, then you would shape it to open the door to get access to the food. The next step would be to place the rat on the elevated platform at the top of the ladder so that it has to "walk the plank" to get to the door. Finally, you would shape ladder climbing to get to the platform. In other words, the idea of backward chaining is first to train the animal to do the last thing in the sequence just before receiving the food. Then you make the opportunity to perform the last

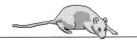

behavior in the sequence contingent on performing the next-to-last behavior, and so on. Most of the complex trained-animal performances that you see in a circus or zoo are achieved through a combination of shaping and backward chaining.

Exercise 5. Extinction

After training Sniffy to press the bar, you might wonder what would happen if you stopped reinforcing bar presses. This sounds like a simple question, but it reflects some of the complexity of life in a world where food sources come and go. Animals need to be flexible. They need to be able to learn what to do to obtain whatever food happens to be available at the moment, and they need to be able to stop doing things that no longer produce food. **Extinction** is the technical name for the behavior changes that occur when a previously reinforced behavior no longer produces reinforcement.

Here is what you need to do to set up and run an extinction experiment:

1. If the Sniffy Lite program is not running, start it.
2. Use the Open command under the File menu to open the file containing your trained Sniffy from Exercise 2.
3. Use the Save As command to save the file under an appropriate new name (for example, Ex5-ext for extinction) on your computer's hard drive. *This step is quite important because it preserves your original trained Sniffy file for future use.* You will need your trained Sniffy file for the next and other exercises.
4. Choose the Design Operant Experiment command from the Experiment menu. Executing this command opens the dialogue box shown at the top of the next page.
5. When the dialogue box opens, the button labeled Continuous is selected because you have been reinforcing all of Sniffy's bar-press responses. Reinforcing every response is a procedure called **continuous reinforcement.**
6. To select extinction, point the cursor at the button labeled Extinction and click your (left) mouse button.
7. Be sure that there is a checkmark in the box next to Mute Pellet Dispenser. (If the checkmark isn't there, place the cursor

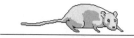

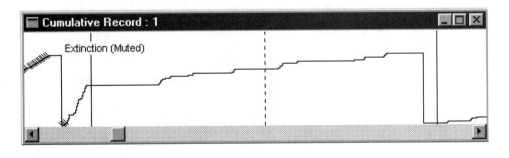

over the box and click your (left) mouse button to put a check-mark in the box.) Setting up extinction with Mute Pellet Dispenser selected means that Sniffy's bar presses will no longer produce food pellets and that he will no longer hear the magazine sound as a consequence of bar pressing. In other words, both the primary reinforcer (food) and the secondary reinforcer (the magazine sound) are turned off. This is the standard extinction procedure.

8. After checking to be sure that you have made the correct setting, click the OK command button.

9. After you click OK, the dialogue box will disappear, and the Sniffy Lite program will begin running again, but Sniffy's bar presses will no longer be reinforced. Immediately after you click OK, your cumulative record will look something like the following.

10. If you want to speed up the experiment, select the Isolate Sniffy (Accelerate Time) command from the Experiment menu.

11. Note that the Sniffy Lite program marks the cumulative record to show the point at which extinction starts and informs you that the magazine is muted.

12. As a consequence of stopping reinforcement, Sniffy's rate of bar pressing will eventually decline until he presses the bar no more often than he did before he was trained. However, the first effect of extinction is to increase Sniffy's bar-pressing rate. This increase in response rate is called an **extinction burst**, and it commonly occurs when an animal is switched from continuous reinforcement to extinction.

13. Your extinction criterion is a 5-minute period during which Sniffy presses the bar no more than twice. When that point is reached, you should save your extinction file by selecting the Save command from the File menu.

14. When the extinction criterion is reached, you should estimate the number of responses that Sniffy made between the onset of extinction and the time when the criterion was reached. You should also estimate the time required to reach the extinction criterion.

15. When estimating the number of responses and the time elapsed during extinction, remember that
    a. The thin, alternating dotted and solid vertical lines on the cumulative record mark off 5-minute periods in program time.
    b. Sniffy always makes 75 responses between two successive pen resets.

16. Determining how many responses Sniffy has made during extinction and the time that extinction required will typically require you to estimate fractional parts of 75-response vertical pen excursions and fractional parts of 5-minute time intervals. You can elect either to make precise measurements or to do "eyeball" estimates.
    a. If you want to make precise measurements, you should print your cumulative record and make the appropriate measurements with a ruler. To print your cumulative record:
        (1) Select the Cumulative Record window by pointing the cursor at it and clicking your (left) mouse button once.
        (2) Select the Print Window command from the File menu.

b. To do an "eyeball" estimate, look at the cumulative record and estimate the appropriate horizontal (time) and vertical (response) movements as a proportion of 5-minute intervals and 75-response vertical pen excursions.

(1) For example, have another look at the cumulative record just shown, which displays the point at which the change from continuous reinforcement to extinction occurred.

(2) The change occurred partway through a 5-minute interval between two vertical lines and partway up from the bottom of the cumulative record.

(3) With regard to time, the change occurred not very long before a vertical line marking the end of a 5-minute interval. Let's say that it occurred about 4/5 or 80 percent of the way through the 5-minute interval. Four-fifths of 5 is 4, so our estimate is that the change occurred about 4 minutes into the 5-minute interval, so that about 1 minute remained before the cumulative record reached the time marker.

(4) With regard to the number of responses that Sniffy made after the previous time marker and before the switch to extinction, it looks as though the cumulative record had moved a little less than 10 percent of the way up from the bottom. Because we know there are 75 responses between pen resets, that means we estimate that Sniffy has made $.1 \times 75$ responses, which is about 7 or 8 responses since the last reset, which in turn means that he had about 70 responses to go before the pen reset again.

A couple of things about the standard extinction experiment are worthy of some discussion. One is the *extinction burst*, the increase in response rate that occurs immediately after Sniffy (or a real rat) is switched from continuous reinforcement to extinction. With real animals, the concept of *frustration* is sometimes evoked as an explanation. An animal that has become accustomed to continuous reinforcement "expects" to be reinforced for every response. When the expected reinforcement fails to occur, frustration, an hypothetical emotional state, results. This emotion supposedly "energizes" the animal to make a burst of responses.

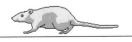

With Sniffy, the explanation is much simpler. Sniffy does not manifest frustration. We know this because we did not model frustration in the Sniffy Lite program. When Sniffy is being maintained on continuous reinforcement, he hears the magazine sound after each bar press and comes down off the bar to eat the pellet of food whose availability the magazine sound signals. When Sniffy is switched to standard extinction, the magazine sound no longer occurs. Without the magazine sound to "call" him from the bar, Sniffy can do several things. He *may* come down off the bar and sniff the food hopper. He *may* also come down off the bar and do other things such as grooming himself or walking around in the operant chamber. However, in the first stages of extinction, the bar-pressing response is still very strong. Thus, the thing Sniffy is most likely to do is to remain mounted at the bar and continue to press the bar again and again. Because Sniffy can press the bar faster if he doesn't come down to examine the food hopper after each bar press, his response rate goes up.

A second thing to note about the standard extinction procedure is that the Operant Associations mind window shows that extinction results in the elimination of the Bar-Sound association. However, the sound-food association remains intact. The Bar-Sound association dissipates because bar presses no longer produce the sound. The Sound-Food association remains intact because Sniffy never hears the sound without receiving a food pellet.

Exercise 6. Secondary Reinforcement

To get Sniffy to bar-press in the first place, you did two things. During magazine training, you turned the magazine sound into a secondary reinforcer by pairing it with food. Then during shaping, you strengthened an association between bar pressing and the sound. Finally, during standard extinction, you turned off both the sound and the food. In this exercise, you will demonstrate the reinforcing power of the magazine sound by leaving it turned on during extinction. In other words, you will set up an extinction experiment in which Sniffy no longer receives any food when he presses the bar. However, bar presses will continue to produce the magazine sound (as if the magazine continued to operate when it contained no food pellets). Presenting the magazine sound as a consequence of bar pressing during extinction will have two effects. First, presenting the sound after each bar press during extinction will for a while continue to reinforce bar presses, with the re-

sult that the extinction process will be slowed down. Second, because the sound occurs but no food pellets are delivered, the Sound-Food association will eventually dissipate.

To set up the experiment, you should follow these steps:

1. If the Sniffy Lite program is not running, start it.
2. Use the Open command under the File menu to open the file containing the Sniffy you trained to bar-press for continuous reinforcement in Exercise 2. (This is the file called Ex2-acq if you followed our file-naming suggestion.)
3. Use the Save As command to save the file under an appropriate new name (such as Ex6-SecRef) on your computer's hard drive. *This step is quite important because it preserves your original trained Sniffy file for future use.* You will need your trained Sniffy for future exercises.
4. Choose the Design Operant Experiment command from the Experiment menu.
5. When the dialogue box opens, point the cursor at the button labeled Extinction and click your (left) mouse button to select that option.
6. Then point the cursor at the box next to Mute Pellet Dispenser and click it to uncheck this option. Setting up extinction with Mute Pellet Dispenser turned off means that Sniffy's bar presses will no longer produce food pellets, but he will continue to hear the magazine sound as a consequence of bar pressing. The primary reinforcer (food) is turned off, but the secondary reinforcer (the magazine sound) remains on.
7. After checking to be sure you have made the correct setting, click the OK command button.
8. After you click OK, the dialogue box will disappear, and the Sniffy Lite program will begin running again. Immediately after clicking OK, your cumulative record will look something like that shown next.

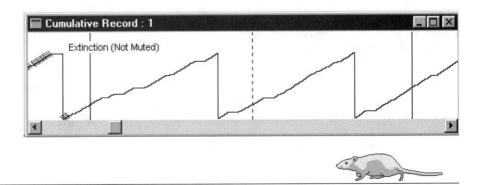

9. If you want to speed up the experiment, select the Isolate Sniffy (Accelerate Time) command from the Experiment menu.

10. Note that the Sniffy Lite program marks the cumulative record to show the point at which extinction starts and informs you that the magazine is not muted.

11. Because Sniffy hears the magazine sound after each bar press, we no longer see the *extinction burst*, the initial increase in the rate of bar pressing, that we saw during standard extinction without the magazine sound. Every time he hears the magazine sound, Sniffy comes down off the bar and sniffs at the food hopper.

12. Your extinction criterion is a 5-minute period during which Sniffy presses the bar no more than twice. When that point is reached, you should save your Secondary Reinforcement file.

13. When the extinction criterion is reached, you should estimate the number of responses that Sniffy made between the onset of extinction and the time when the criterion was reached and the time required to reach the extinction criterion.

14. You should compare Sniffy's extinction with the magazine sound turned on with the extinction you observed in the previous exercise. This comparison will reveal that Sniffy makes more responses and that the extinction process takes more time when the magazine sound remains on than when it is muted. This difference is caused by the initial secondary reinforcing power of the magazine sound when it occurs during extinction.

15. Finally, note that after extinction with the magazine sound turned on, the Sound-Food association extinguished, but the Bar-Sound association did not. The Sound-Food association dissipates because the sound occurs but no food pellet is presented. The Bar-Sound association remains intact because Sniffy continues to hear the sound after each bar press.

Exercise 7. Spontaneous Recovery

A single extinction session is not enough to permanently reduce the frequency of an operant response to its pretraining frequency. If an animal that has apparently been fully extinguished is removed from the

operant chamber, allowed to rest in its home cage for 24 hours, and then returned to the operant chamber for a second extinction session, its response rate at the start of the second session will be greater than it was at the end of the first extinction session. This rest-produced reappearance of an extinguished operant response is called **spontaneous recovery.**

To simulate the phenomenon with Sniffy:

1. Open a file in which Sniffy has been trained to press the bar and then extinguished. Either your Ex5-ext or your Ex6-SecRef file will work for this purpose.
2. Use the Save As command to save the file under a new appropriate name (for example, Ex7-SponRec) on your computer's hard drive.
3. Choose Remove Sniffy for Time-Out from the Experiment menu. To simulate taking a rest, Sniffy will disappear momentarily and then reappear.
4. When he reappears, his bar-pressing rate will be higher than it was at the end of extinction, but lower than it was before extinction. Immediately after the time-out, your cumulative record should resemble that shown next.

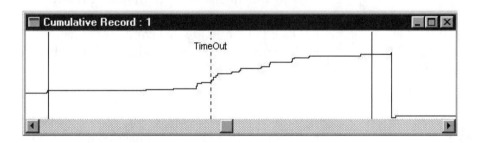

5. If you want to speed up the experiment, select the Isolate Sniffy (Accelerate Time) command from the Experiment menu.
6. Check the Operant Associations mind window shortly after starting your spontaneous recovery experiment. You'll recall that standard extinction (with the magazine sound muted) extinguishes the Bar-Sound association, whereas extinction with the magazine sound not muted extinguishes the Sound-Food association. At the beginning of the spontaneous recovery experiment, the extinguished association is partly restored. This

partial reappearance of the extinguished association is the "psychological" reason why Sniffy presses the bar more often at the beginning of the second extinction session than he did at the end of the first extinction session.

7. Let the Sniffy Lite program run until Sniffy meets the extinction criterion again.

8. Compare the number of responses made and the time required to reach the extinction criterion during this second extinction session with the number of responses and time required during the first extinction session. This comparison will reveal that the second time around Sniffy makes fewer responses and takes less time to reach the criterion.

Copying and Pasting the Contents of a Sniffy Lite Window

Let's imagine that your professor wants you to write a lab report describing the results of one of your Sniffy Lite experiments and that you want to include a picture of some of your results in the report. To create a picture of one of the Sniffy Lite windows, follow these steps:

- Open the Sniffy file that contains the data you want to display.
- If necessary, make the window you want to display visible by selecting it from the Windows menu.
- Once the window is visible, make sure that it is the "active window" by pointing the cursor at some part of the window and clicking your (left) mouse button once.
- Select the Copy Window Image command from the Edit menu.
- Open your word processor file to the place where you want to insert the picture. You probably want to insert the picture into a blank paragraph.
- Select the Paste or Paste Special command from the word processor's Edit menu.
- A picture of the window appears in your word processor document.
- The picture contains the contents of the window as it was displayed in the Sniffy Lite program at the time you executed the Copy Window Image command. The title bar and borders of the window are omitted.

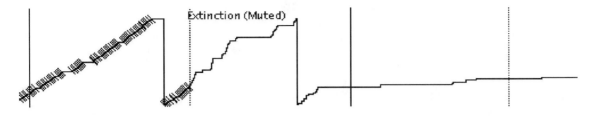

- If your computer has enough random-access memory (RAM), you can have your word processor program and Sniffy Lite running at the same time, a setup that is very convenient. If your computer does not have enough RAM to run both programs simultaneously, you will need to quit (exit from) Sniffy Lite before opening the word processor file that contains your report.

4 Schedules of Reinforcement and the Partial-Reinforcement Effect

Background and Examples

In extinction, reinforcement is completely cut off. This action simulates the situation in which a once-available food source has ceased to exist. Another even more common real-world scenario is one in which a response is sometimes reinforced and sometimes not reinforced. When a wild rat searches for food, there is no guarantee that it will find it in the same place every time. The rat's searches are based on the probability of locating food. Going to a location where there once was food and finding none would not necessarily discourage the rat from trying there again at some other time when food might be available.

In a similar way, consider what your reaction might be if you turned on a light switch and the light failed to come on. How you would react would likely depend on your previous experience with that light switch. If the switch had worked reliably in the past, you would probably immediately go to look for a new lightbulb. However, if the switch had sometimes required several flicks before the light came on, you would probably spend some time flicking it on and off before you decided that this time the problem was likely a burnt-out bulb.

With regard to Sniffy, so far we have discussed reinforcement as something that either occurs every time Sniffy presses the bar or not at all. However, you can also choose to reinforce only some of Sniffy's bar presses. The technical name for reinforcing every instance of a target behavior is **continuous reinforcement (CRF).** The technical term for reinforcing some, but not all, instances of a behavior is **partial reinforcement (PRF).** A rule that determines which instances of a response to reinforce is called a **schedule of reinforcement.** PRF schedules affect the temporal patterning of responses as viewed on a cumulative record. In

addition, PRF schedules enhance resistance to extinction. By enhanced resistance to extinction, we mean that, if a response has been reinforced on a PRF schedule, the animal will make more responses during extinction than would be the case if the response had always been reinforced (continuous reinforcement).

The comparative effects of partial and continuous reinforcement on resistance to extinction can have real-life implications. Suppose that you are a parent of a young child. Many children who are about 2 years old develop a tendency to exhibit temper tantrums. In fact, this problem is so common that children in that age group are sometimes called the "terrible twos." How parents react to tantrums can have a profound influence on the duration of this "phase" of their child's development.

When a child has a tantrum, you can either reinforce the tantrum behavior by giving the child what he or she wants or not reinforce the behavior by letting the child kick and scream until he or she gets tired and stops. (We assume you are not a person who would spank a child for tantrum behavior.) The best advice to parents of children who are just beginning to have tantrums is never to reinforce the behavior. If you never reinforce a tantrum, your child should pass through this phase quickly. However, many parents end up giving in to the child, especially if a tantrum occurs in public. The findings of operant conditioning suggest that if you are going to reinforce the behavior, it is better to do so consistently. That way, when the time comes to extinguish the behavior, the process should be faster than if you sometimes let the child scream and sometimes give the child what he or she wants.

Continuous reinforcement is the most efficient way to shape a new behavior quickly. But once the target behavior has been conditioned, continuous reinforcement is no longer necessary. Imagine the nursery school teacher's task with a new class of children. There are a great many new things the students need to learn, not only the prescribed lessons but also social skills that will allow them to participate in the classroom. In the beginning, the teacher needs to reinforce the children's appropriate behaviors as often as possible. The teacher dispenses praise, stickers, and certificates and stamps stars on their hands. The nursery school teacher is a dispenser of reinforcers who at first must provide as close to a continuous-reinforcement schedule as is possible. However, this level of reinforcement is impossible to maintain, and children are soon exposed to a partial reinforcement schedule. In first grade, children who know an answer to a question are expected to raise their hands and wait to be called on, and not every raised hand is recognized. As long as each child gets occasional recognition, the skills they have learned will not disappear because with partial reinforcement it is difficult to extinguish their learned behaviors.

As noted earlier, a schedule of reinforcement is a rule for determining which responses to reinforce. In their book *Schedules of Reinforcement*, C. B. Ferster and B. F. Skinner (1957) describe many different possible schedules. However, all the described schedules are made of combinations of two basic "families" of schedules: **ratio schedules** and **interval schedules.**

Ratio schedules reinforce the subject for making some particular number of responses. On a **fixed-ratio (FR) schedule,** the number of responses required is always the same. On an FR-5 schedule, the subject must make five responses for each reinforcement. This is rather like being paid for piecework, where the amount of money earned depends on the amount of work accomplished according to a prearranged pay scale. Because the amount of money earned is directly proportional to the amount of work performed, piecework tends to produce high rates of output.

When we observe animals on an FR schedule in the operant chamber, the pattern of performance seen on the cumulative record depends on the size of the ratio. Small FR schedules, which require only a small number of responses for each reinforcement, produce fast, steady responding. However, the performance of an animal that is being maintained on a large FR schedule is characterized by a pause after the receipt of each reinforcement, followed by an abrupt transition to rapid, steady responding until the next reinforcement occurs. As the size of a large FR schedule is increased, the pause after each reinforcement becomes longer. We can see something that resembles this pattern of responding in the behavior of a student who finds it difficult to start the next task after finishing a major assignment. The student's behavior is affected by the fact that a lot more work is required before the next reinforcement is obtained.

On a **variable-ratio (VR) schedule**, the value of the schedule specifies an average number of responses required to obtain reinforcement, but the exact number of responses varies from reinforcement to reinforcement. On a VR-5 schedule, the subject must make five responses on average for each reinforcement. Sometimes the subject must make eight or ten responses before reinforcement occurs, but these large values are balanced by occasions when reinforcement occurs after only one or two responses. VR schedules typically produce high rates of responding with no long pauses.

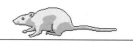

VR schedules are common in everyday life. Las Vegas–style slot machines pay off on a VR schedule, as does trying to arrange a date for Saturday night, or selling something on a commission basis. In all these situations, there is some chance or probability of success associated with every "response" that you make. The more often you respond, the more often you will be reinforced.

Interval schedules reinforce the subject for the first response made after a specified time interval has elapsed since the last reinforcement was received. The time period during which reinforcement is unavailable begins when the subject receives a reinforcer. The interval thus specifies a minimum amount of time that must elapse between reinforced responses. On a **fixed-interval (FI) schedule,** the interval that must elapse before another response will be reinforced is always the same. On an FI-60 sec schedule, exactly 60 seconds must always elapse after the receipt of one reinforcer before another response will be reinforced.

If your school is typical, every class period ends at a specified time. If you observe your fellow students, you will notice that their behavior changes as the time approaches when the class is scheduled to end. Early in the class period, everyone listens fairly attentively; and many students busily take notes. However, as the end of class approaches, students begin to put their notes away and prepare to leave.

On a **variable-interval (VI) schedule,** the time interval following reinforcement that must elapse before the next response is reinforced varies from reinforcement to reinforcement. On a VI-10 sec schedule, the time interval would average 10 seconds. Few, if any, real-life situations are exactly equivalent to VI scheduling in the laboratory. However, trying to telephone someone whose line is frequently busy is similar to reinforcement on a VI schedule. Your call won't go through until the line is free, and the line is busy for varying periods. The difference is that on a pure VI schedule, once the time interval has elapsed, the reinforcer becomes available and remains available until the subject responds; but when you are trying to call an often busy telephone number, the line is busy and free intermittently. You can miss chances to complete the call by not trying often enough.

Each of these simple schedules produces a characteristic performance from subjects maintained on the schedule long enough for their behavior to stabilize. Depending on which schedule is involved, the animal may press the bar at a steady, predictable rate; or its response rate may vary in predictable ways. Prior to the appearance of the characteristic pattern of responding associated with the schedule, there is a period of acquisition during which the animal gradually adjusts to the schedule.

Variable-Ratio (VR) and Variable-Interval (VI) Schedules

Both variable-ratio (VR) and variable-interval (VI) schedules produce steady responding, but at different rates. VR schedules produce fast, steady responding. VI schedules produce slow, steady responding.

The difference between the performances maintained by VR and VI schedules is nicely illustrated in an experiment described by Reynolds (1975). The experiment involved two pigeons pecking at disks for food reinforcement in separate operant chambers. The experiment involved a **yoked experimental design,** which means that the behavior of the first pigeon could affect the other bird's reinforcement schedule. In the first chamber, pigeon A's disk pecking was reinforced on a VR schedule that the experimenter had programmed. In the other, completely isolated chamber, pigeon B's disk pecking was reinforced on a VI schedule in which the values of the intervals were determined by pigeon A's behavior. Each time pigeon A received a reinforcer for completing a ratio, a reinforcer became available for pigeon B's next response.

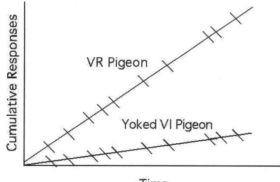

Idealized performances of two pigeons in yoked operant chambers. Both birds peck steadily. However, although both birds receive the same number of reinforcements at virtually the same instants, the VR bird makes many more responses.

This graph shows hypothetical cumulative records generated by two birds in this kind of experiment. Note that both birds respond at a nearly constant rate, but the bird on the VR schedule responds faster

than the bird on the VI schedule. Although both birds' pecking behaviors are reinforced at virtually the same instant and although both always receive the same amount of reinforcement, there is a distinct difference in the rate at which they peck. This difference is due to differences in the way in which the schedules interact with the birds' pecking behavior.

Fixed-Ratio (FR) Schedules

As shown in the next figure, the typical FR performance depends on the size of the ratio—that is, on the fixed number of responses required for each reinforcement. What constitutes a small ratio depends on the organism and the effort required in making the response. For Sniffy and other rats pressing a bar, a small ratio is anything requiring up to 10 or 15 bar presses. For a pigeon pecking an illuminated disk, a small ratio is anything up to about 50. With small ratios, the performance is quite steady with no pause after each reinforcement. With large ratios, there is a pause after each reinforcement, followed by an abrupt transition to a high, stable rate until the next reinforcer is received.

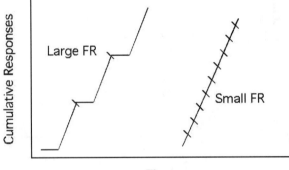

Idealized performances maintained by large and small FR schedules.

Fixed-Interval (FI) Schedules

Overall, FI schedules maintain rather slow rates of responding, more or less comparable to those maintained by VI schedules. However, whereas the VI performance is steady, the typical FI performance in-

volves a pause after the receipt of each reinforcement, followed by a gradually accelerating response rate until the subject is responding moderately fast just before the next reinforcement is due. This typical FI response pattern, an idealized version of which is depicted in the next figure, is often called the **FI scallop.** As is the case with FR schedules, the pauses that occur after the receipt of a reinforcer are much more pronounced on large FI schedules than on small FI schedules.

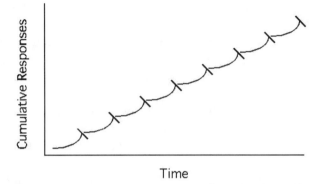

Idealized performances maintained by an FI schedule.

Setting Up a Schedule in the Design Operant Experiment Dialogue Box

Let's consider how to set up schedule experiments in Sniffy Lite. You establish different reinforcement schedules by choosing the Design Operant Experiment command from the Experiment menu. When you execute this command, the following dialogue box appears.

Here is how the dialogue box works:

- The Fixed and Variable alternatives determine whether the schedule requirements will be fixed or variable.
- The buttons labeled Responses and Seconds determine whether Sniffy is on a ratio or interval schedule.
    - Choosing Responses sets up a ratio schedule.
    - Choosing Seconds sets up an interval schedule.
- You set the value of the schedule (the number of responses required or the number of seconds after a reinforcement before another response can be reinforced) by typing a number into the text box.
- For example, if you wanted to set up a VI-20 sec schedule, you would select the Variable and Seconds alternatives and type 20 in the text box.
- Selecting the button labeled Continuous sets up continuous reinforcement. All Sniffy's bar presses are reinforced. This setting is the default in effect whenever you create a new, untrained Sniffy file.
- Selecting the button labeled Extinction sets up an extinction condition. If there is a checkmark in the box labeled Mute Pellet Dispenser, the magazine sound is turned off during extinction. This is the usual way extinction is studied. If there is no checkmark in the box labeled Mute Pellet Dispenser, Sniffy continues to hear the magazine sound whenever he presses the bar even though he no longer receives a food pellet. As we saw in Chapter 3, this nonstandard extinction setting enables you to study the secondary reinforcing power of the magazine sound.
- When you click the OK button after setting up a reinforcement schedule, the dialogue box disappears, and the Sniffy Lite program starts reinforcing Sniffy according to the schedule you established.
- When you click Cancel, the dialogue box disappears and the program continues reinforcing Sniffy according to whatever schedule was in effect before you opened the dialogue box. None of the settings that you made while the dialogue box was open are implemented.

Exercise 8. Placing Sniffy on a Small VR Schedule

Here are the steps to follow to place Sniffy on a small variable-ratio (VR) schedule of reinforcement. Except for the settings in the Design Operant Experiment dialogue box, you would follow the same steps to place Sniffy on any small-value schedule.

1. Before Sniffy can be placed on a schedule, he must first be trained to press the bar for continuous reinforcement.
   a. If you still have the file that you created after first training Sniffy to press the bar in Exercise 2 (the file that we suggested you call Ex2-acq), use the Open command in the File menu to open the file.
   b. If you do not have your original trained Sniffy file, you can use the file called CRF, which is located in the Sample Files folder that the Sniffy Lite Installer program placed inside the Sniffy Lite for Windows or Sniffy Lite for Macintosh folder on your computer's hard drive.
   c. Look at the Operant Associations mind window. (If necessary, make the Operant Associations window visible by selecting it from the Mind Windows section of the Windows menu.) Make sure that both the Sound-Food and Bar-Sound associations are at their maximum levels. If you have opened your own file and discover that one or both of these associations is below its maximum level, you can let the program run until both associations reach their maximums before going on to the next step. If you are in a hurry, copy the CRF file from the Sample Files folder.
2. Select the Save As command from the File menu to give the file an appropriate new name and save it on your computer's hard drive. *This step is important because it preserves your original CRF-trained Sniffy for use in other experiments.* In this example we will be creating a file in which Sniffy is trained to respond on a VR-5 schedule, so we suggest that you call the new file Ex8-VR5.
3. Choose the Design Operant Experiments command from the Experiment menu. Select the Variable and Responses alternatives. Type 5 in the text box. Click OK.
4. If you want to speed up the experiment, select the Isolate Sniffy (Accelerate Time) command from the Experiment menu.
5. Shortly after the Design Operant Experiment dialogue box closes, your Cumulative Record window will look something like the one shown at the top of the next page. Note that the Sniffy Lite program marks the point at which the VR-5 schedule was introduced.
6. Immediately after being switched onto a schedule when Sniffy encounters unreinforced responding for the first time, he will

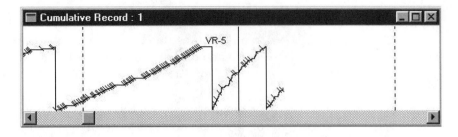

begin to extinguish. The Operant Associations mind window will display this process as a decrease in the strength of the Bar-Sound association. If Sniffy is fully trained on CRF before you place him on a VR-5 schedule, he will not extinguish fully. However, if his CRF training were incomplete, or if you tried to place him on a schedule with too large an initial value (for example, VR-25), he would very likely extinguish.

7. If Sniffy is going to adjust successfully to the schedule on which you have placed him, the Bar-Sound association will begin to increase again after Sniffy has received several reinforcements on the schedule.

8. Sniffy is completely trained on the schedule when the Bar-Sound association reaches its maximum. At that point, Sniffy's cumulative record will be displaying the response pattern typical of the schedule on which Sniffy is being maintained.

9. When the Bar-Sound association reaches its maximum, choose the Save command from the File menu to save your file.

Exercise 9. Increasing the Value of Sniffy's VR Schedule

Sniffy can be trained to respond on schedules with quite high values (such as VR-400 or FI-300 sec) provided these high values are approached gradually through intermediate stages. Here are the steps that you go through to increase the value of a schedule. For the sake of illustration, we will assume you are going to increase the value of the VR-5 schedule from the previous exercise.

1. If the Sniffy Lite program is not running, start it.
2. Use the Open command under the File menu to open your VR-5 file.

3. Check the Operant Associations mind window to be sure that the Bar-Sound association is at its maximum level. If it isn't, let the program run until Bar-Sound association reaches its maximum.

4. Select the Save As command from the File menu and save the file under an appropriate name on your computer's hard drive. Because we are going to be increasing the value of Sniffy's VR-5 schedule to VR-10, we suggest you call the new file Ex9-VR10. Saving the new file under a different name preserves your original VR-5 file for future use.

5. Select the Design Operant Experiment command from the Experiment menu. Be sure the Variable and Responses alternatives are selected, type the number 10 in the text box, and click OK.

6. If you want to speed up the experiment, select the Isolate Sniffy (Accelerate Time) command from the Experiment menu.

7. Because Sniffy is now experiencing longer runs of unreinforced trials, the Bar-Sound association will weaken at first. However, after Sniffy has received several reinforcements on the new schedule, the Bar-Sound association will start going back up. When it reaches its maximum again, choose the Save command from the File menu to preserve your VR-10 trained Sniffy.

8. Repeat relevant parts of the instructions given in Steps 4 through 6 to shape Sniffy up to a VR-50 schedule.

   a. Sniffy will easily and quickly reach the VR-50 endpoint if you use VR-20 and VR-35 as your intermediate steps.

   b. If you like to live dangerously, try stepping Sniffy up to a VR-50 after VR-10 or VR-20. He may or may not extinguish with these larger steps.

9. The cumulative record you obtain once Sniffy has fully adapted to the VR-50 schedule should resemble the following. Note the rapid, reasonably steady response pattern.

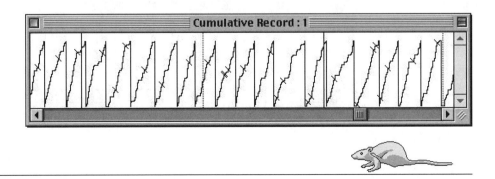

Exercise 10. Variable-Interval Schedules

1. Follow the generalized instructions given in Exercise 9 to shape Sniffy up to a VI-50 sec schedule.
2. If you want to speed up the experiment, select the Isolate Sniffy (Accelerate Time) command from the Experiment menu.
3. The cumulative record that you obtain once Sniffy has fully adapted to the VI-50 schedule should resemble the following. Note the slow, reasonably steady response pattern.

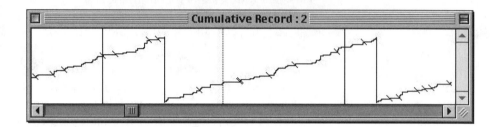

Exercise 11. Fixed-Ratio Schedules

1. Follow the generalized instructions given in Exercise 9 to shape Sniffy up to an FR-50 schedule.
2. If you want to speed up the experiment, select the Isolate Sniffy (Accelerate Time) command from the Experiment menu.
3. The cumulative record that you obtain once Sniffy has fully adapted to the FR-50 schedule should resemble the following. Note the pauses in responding that occur after each reinforcement is received and the abrupt transitions to rapid responding at the end of each pause.

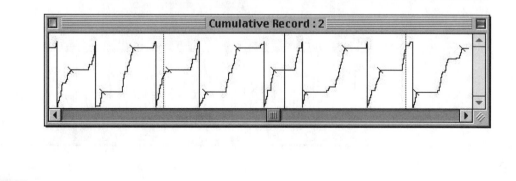

Exercise 12. Fixed-Interval Schedules

1. Follow the generalized instructions given in Exercise 9 to shape Sniffy up to a FI-50 sec schedule.
2. If you want to speed up the experiment, select the Isolate Sniffy (Accelerate Time) command from the Experiment menu.
3. The cumulative record that you obtain once Sniffy has fully adapted to the FI-50 schedule should resemble the following. Note the pauses after each reinforcement is received, followed by rather gradual transitions to moderate response rates shortly before the next reinforcement is due to occur.

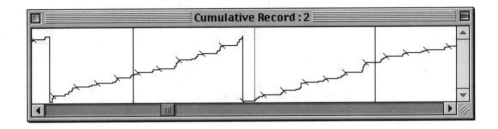

How Realistic Are Sniffy's Schedule Performances?

The speed with which Sniffy adapts to reinforcement schedules is one of the places where we sacrificed realism for convenience. Real rats adapt to schedules slowly. In many instances, a real rat requires several daily one-hour training sessions before its pattern of responding in the cumulative record begins to resemble the response pattern that a particular schedule "typically" produces. Sniffy adapts to schedules and schedule changes much faster—within no more than an hour, and sometimes within a few minutes of program time. We speeded up Sniffy's learning process so that you will have the opportunity to look at the effects of many different schedules in a reasonable amount of time.

Sniffy's schedule performances are not perfect replicas of the idealized schedule performances shown in the first part of this chapter and in many textbooks on the psychology of learning. Idealized performances are designed to communicate ideas about what psychologists think schedule performances would look like if all the "noise" could

be averaged out. The actual performances you obtain with Sniffy and the actual performances of real rats are rarely ideal because the factors that tend to produce ideal performances are not the only things determining the animal's behavior. For example, VR schedules are supposed to produce rapid, steady responding, and they tend to do so. However, pressing the bar is not the only thing rats do while being reinforced on a VR schedule. Sometimes they take drinks of water. Sometimes they groom or scratch themselves. Sometimes they wander around the operant chamber for a little while. All these interruptions make actual VR performances less rapid and especially less steady than they would be if the only factors involved were those discussed in the first parts of this chapter.

Thus, the fact that Sniffy's cumulative records are not perfect replicas of ideal schedule performances means that, to a degree, Sniffy is behaving like a real rat. If you look at reproductions of the actual performances of real rats in scientific journal articles and in specialized books on reinforcement schedules, you will discover that Sniffy's schedule performances fall within the range of performances that real rats sometimes produce.

Exercise 13. The Effect of Partial Reinforcement on Extinction

Partial reinforcement dramatically increases a response's resistance to extinction. Animals whose responding has been maintained by a partial-reinforcement schedule make many more responses during extinction than do animals whose responding has been maintained on continuous reinforcement. In addition, ratio schedules tend to produce greater resistance to extinction than interval schedules; and variable schedules tend to produce greater resistance to extinction than fixed schedules. The Sniffy Lite program enables you to observe these differences in resistance to extinction. To measure Sniffy's resistance to extinction following partial reinforcement, follow these steps:

1. Open a Sniffy Lite file in which Sniffy has been fully trained to respond on a moderate- or large-value schedule. We suggest that you use a file in which you have trained Sniffy to respond on a schedule with a value of at least 25 (that is, VR-25, FR-25, VI-25 sec, or FI-25 sec).

2. Look at the Operant Associations mind window to verify that Bar-Sound association is at its maximum level.

3. Save the file under an appropriate new name (for example, Ex13-VR25Ext) to preserve your original schedule file for future use.

4. Choose the Design Operant Experiment command from the Experiment menu.

5. Click the Extinction option in the dialogue box, make sure that there is a checkmark in the box next to Mute Pellet Dispenser, and click the OK command button.

6. If you want to speed up the experiment, select the Isolate Sniffy (Accelerate Time) command from the Experiment menu.

7. Let the program run until Sniffy reaches the extinction criterion of no more than two responses during a 5-minute period.

8. Save the file.

9. Print the cumulative record and determine how many responses Sniffy made and how much time elapsed before he reached the extinction criterion.

10. Compare your partial-reinforcement extinction results with the extinction results that you obtained earlier when Sniffy's responding had been maintained by continuous reinforcement.

5

Introduction to Classical Conditioning

Background

Classical conditioning is the form of learning that results when two stimuli reliably occur in a sequence so that the first stimulus predicts the occurrence of the second. Usually, the stimuli have differing degrees of biological importance to the organism, with the less important stimulus preceding the more important stimulus. Many of the phenomena of classical conditioning were first described by the Russian physiologist Ivan Pavlov and his associates, who were the first to explore this form of learning systematically (Pavlov, 1927). Two other names for the same kind of learning are **Pavlovian conditioning** and **respondent conditioning.**

In classical conditioning, the stimulus that comes first in the temporal sequence is called the **conditioned stimulus (CS),** and the stimulus that comes second is called the **unconditioned stimulus (US).** The US initially possesses the capacity to elicit an obvious, easy-to-measure response called the **unconditioned response (UR).** The initial response to the CS is called the **orienting response (OR),** but the OR is often so inconspicuous that psychologists treat the CS as if it were a neutral stimulus that initially elicits no response at all. In other words, the OR to the CS is rarely measured.

The **classical conditioning acquisition procedure** consists of repeatedly presenting the CS shortly before the US. As a consequence of this repeated pairing of the two stimuli, the CS gradually acquires the capacity to elicit a new learned response, which is called the **conditioned response (CR).** Usually, but not always, the CR resembles the UR in the sense that the CR consists of certain components of the UR. When a response component that occurs in both the CR and UR is measured quantitatively, the response magnitude in the CR is usually smaller.

In their early experiments, Pavlov and his associates used food placed in the mouths of food-deprived dogs as the US. Food in a hungry dog's mouth elicits chewing, swallowing, and salivation as a UR. As CSs, Pavlov's group used various medium-intensity sounds, lights, and tactile stimuli, none of which had any initial tendency to elicit a response resembling the UR to food. When repeatedly paired with food presentation, all these CSs gradually acquired the capacity to elicit salivation. During the more than 90 years since Pavlov first reported his findings, thousands of classical conditioning experiments have been performed, employing dozens of different species and a wide variety of different stimuli as US and CS.

The Conditioned Emotional Response (CER)

Sniffy Lite simulates a form of classical conditioning called the **conditioned emotional response (CER)** or **conditioned suppression**, which was first described by Estes and Skinner (1941). In this procedure, a rat is first trained to bar-press for food reinforcement on a schedule of reinforcement that produces steady responding (such as a moderate-sized VR schedule). The rat's steady response rate is then used as a baseline against which to measure the effects of presenting stimuli.

Sudden, intense sounds and electric shocks delivered to a rat's feet are stimuli that intrinsically possess the capacity to interrupt a rat's steady bar pressing. Thus, these stimuli can be used as USs. In contrast, less intense sounds and lights initially have little or no effect on a rat's response rate. For this reason, these stimuli can be used as CSs. The conditioning procedure consists of turning on the stimulus that is serving as the CS for a period of time before briefly presenting the US. Usually, the CS and US terminate simultaneously. In different experiments, the period of time during each trial when the CS is presented by itself typically ranges between 30 and 120 seconds (Mazur, 1998; Domjan, 1998). The duration of the US is usually 1 second or less. As a consequence of pairing the CS with the US, the CS gradually acquires the capacity to suppress bar pressing.

Over the past 20 years or so, the CER has become the form of classical conditioning that North American psychologists most commonly study. There are probably two main reasons for this popularity. First, the CER provides an experimental preparation for studying the acquisition of a very important and interesting response—fear. Second, because the entire process of presenting stimuli and collecting data can be fully automated, the CER is a very convenient form of classical conditioning to study.

To measure the CR to the CS in CER experiments, psychologists employ a response measure called the **suppression ratio**. The basic idea behind the suppression ratio is to compare the rate of bar pressing (the number of bar presses per minute) during the CS (rate during CS) to the rate of bar pressing during the period of time immediately preceding presentation of the CS (rate pre CS). When the pre-CS and during-CS time periods are of equal duration (as in Sniffy Lite), comparing the bar-pressing rates is equivalent to comparing the number of bar presses during the CS (bar presses during CS) to the number of bar presses during the period preceding the CS (bar presses pre CS). If the CS elicits no fear response, the number of bar presses during these two time periods should be about the same. However, if the CS suppresses bar pressing, then bar presses during CS will be less than bar presses pre CS. To get a quantitative measure of the suppression of bar pressing in response to the CS, the suppression ratio is expressed as the ratio between the bar presses during CS and the sum of bar presses during CS plus bar presses pre CS. Written as an equation, the suppression ratio is defined as:

$$\text{Suppression ratio} = \frac{\text{Bar Presses During CS}}{\text{Bar Presses During CS} + \text{Bar Presses Pre CS}}$$

Let's think a bit about how this equation works. If presenting the CS does not affect the animal's bar pressing (that is, if bar presses during CS = bar presses pre CS), then the denominator of the fraction will be twice as large as the numerator; and the suppression ratio will be 0.5. However, if the CS suppresses bar pressing so that the rat presses less during the CS than during the pre-CS period, the suppression ratio will be less than 0.5; and if the rat doesn't press the bar at all during the CS, the suppression ratio will be zero. In a CER experiment where the CS is being paired with an aversive US, bar presses during CS should never (except by chance) be greater than bar presses pre CS, so that the suppression ratio should generally be less than or equal to 0.5. On the first training trial (before the animal has experienced the US), the suppression ratio should be about 0.5. Then as conditioning proceeds, the value of the suppression ratio should decline until it eventually levels off at an average value less than 0.5.

With real rats and in the Sniffy Lite program, CER conditioning is rather rapid. The suppression ratio usually levels out at a minimal value after 10 or fewer CS–US pairings. The Sniffy Lite program compares Sniffy's response rate during the 30 seconds preceding each CS

presentation with his response rate during the 30 seconds that each CS lasts.[1]

The US that the Sniffy Lite program simulates is electric foot shock delivered through the parallel metal bars that form the floor of Sniffy's operant chamber. Shock duration is always 1 second. Shocking Sniffy immediately interrupts his bar-pressing performance. He jumps and then freezes. When he begins to move around again, bouts of freezing are interspersed with bouts of grooming and exploratory behavior. After about 2 minutes, the effect of the shock wears off, and he returns to bar pressing.

To animate Sniffy's UR to the shock US, we applied some tricks to sequences of animation frames derived from a videotape of a rat that had *not* been shocked or exposed to any other form of noxious stimulation. We think that the result looks plausible, but we do not know how realistic it is. Psychologists who study the CER typically report their results as suppression ratios and virtually never give detailed descriptions of their animals' UR to the US. The Sniffy Lite program simulates typical suppression ratio results. To create a realistic simulation of a rat's response to shock, we would have had to videotape a rat that was actually being shocked, but we did not do that.

The CS that the Sniffy Lite program employs is a light. Duration of the CS is always 30 seconds. On trials when the CS is paired with the US, the US occurs during the last second of the CS. In other words, the onset of the CS always precedes the onset of the US by 29 seconds.[2] The light initially has no effect on Sniffy's bar-pressing performance. However, when a light is paired with the shock US, the light gradually acquires the capacity to suppress bar pressing as a CR. When he is fully conditioned, Sniffy will begin showing bouts of freezing, grooming, and exploratory behavior soon after the light comes on. As was the case with the UR, although we think that Sniffy's CR looks plausible, we do not know how realistic it is because we did not videotape a rat that was actually being conditioned to manifest a CER.

The Design Classical Conditioning Experiment Dialogue Box

As noted earlier, one of the reasons for the CER's popularity with North American researchers is the fact that all aspects of CER experiments can be automated. A computer controls the presentation of

[1] As usual, all times given are in Sniffy Lite program time.
[2] All these times refer to Sniffy Lite program time.

stimuli, records the rat's bar-pressing responses, and computes the suppression ratio. The Sniffy Lite program provides you with a simple interface that enables you to set up and run basic classical conditioning experiments. Like a psychologist in a research lab, you will set up the experiment and then let your computer perform the experiment and collect the data. When you choose the Design Classical Conditioning Experiment command from the Experiment menu, the following dialogue box appears:

Classical Conditioning Experiment Design

Stage

View/Edit Experiment Stage   1

Next Stage	Previous Stage	Interval Between Trials [5] Minutes
New Stage	Delete Stage	Number of Trials [1]

First Stimulus

Light

Second Stimulus

- ● Shock US
- ○ None

[Cancel]   [Save]

- Classical conditioning experiments can contain one or more **stages**. A stage is a group of trials. All the trials in one stage are run before any of the trials in the next stage.
- In the Stage section of the dialogue box, the number after View/Edit Experiment Stage indicates which stage of the experiment you are currently viewing. When you first open the dialogue box by selecting the Design Classical Conditioning Experiment command from the Experiment menu, the numeral to the right of View/Edit Experiment Stage will always be 1, indicating that Stage 1 of the experiment is being displayed.
- You can edit (create or change) any stage that has not already been run, and you can add more stages to an experiment in which one or more early stages have already been run. You can also view the settings for stages that have been run. However, you cannot change the

settings for any stage that has already been run or for a stage that is in the process of being run. When you view the settings for a stage that has already been run or for the stage currently being run, all command buttons are dimmed, and you cannot enter any information into the text boxes.

- The Stage section of the dialogue box contains four command buttons and two boxes into which you can type numerals.

- If you are viewing or editing Stage 1 of an experiment, the **Previous Stage** command button is dimmed. However, if you are working on Stage 2 or higher, the Previous Stage command is available. Executing the command by clicking your (left) mouse button while pointing at the command button will move you to the previous stage. For example, if you were working on Stage 3, clicking on the Previous Stage button would move you back to Stage 2, and clicking it a second time would move you back to Stage 1.

- The **Next Stage** button moves you from stage to stage in the opposite direction. For example, if you have created three stages and are currently working on Stage 2, clicking the Next Stage button moves you to Stage 3. The Next Stage button is dimmed when you are viewing or working on the last stage that you have defined.

- Clicking on the **New Stage** button creates a new stage, inserts it immediately after the stage that you were viewing when you clicked the button, and automatically moves you to the new stage. If necessary, other stages of the experiment are automatically renumbered. For example, if you have already created three stages and are currently working on Stage 2, clicking on New Stage will create a new Stage 3 and insert it between Stage 2 and the stage that was previously called Stage 3. The former Stage 3 automatically becomes Stage 4.

- The **Delete Stage** button deletes the current stage and, if necessary, automatically renumbers the other stages. Suppose that you have already defined four stages in an experiment and are currently working on Stage 3. Clicking the Delete Stage button will eliminate the old Stage 3 and cause the stage that had previously been called Stage 4 to be renumbered as Stage 3.

- You specify the average time interval between trials for the current stage by typing a number into the **Interval Between Trials** text box. Intervals between trials are measured in minutes. The number you type must be an integer (a whole number without a decimal point). The shortest allowable average interval is 2 minutes; the longest is 20 minutes. Remember that you are specifying the *average* interval between trials. The actual intervals vary from trial to trial so that Sniffy cannot learn to anticipate when the next CS is going to occur.

- The number you type into the box labeled **Number of Trials** determines the number of trials in the stage you are currently editing.
- Below the Stage section of the dialogue box are sections for defining the First Stimulus (CS) and Second Stimulus (the stimulus, if any, that comes after the CS).
- In Sniffy Lite, the first stimulus is always the light CS, and the duration of the light is always 30 seconds of Sniffy program time.
- There are two possible Second Stimulus settings: Shock US and None.
- Selecting the Shock US alternative causes the shock to follow every occurrence of the light during the stage that you are currently editing.
- Selecting the None second stimulus alternative causes the light CS to occur without the shock on each trial of the stage you are currently editing.

The following two command buttons appear at the bottom of the Classical Conditioning Experimental Design dialogue box:

- Choosing **Cancel** closes the Classical Conditioning Experimental Design dialogue box without saving any of the experimental design settings or changes that you have made.
- Choosing **Save** saves the experimental design you have created (or any changes that you have made to the design) as a part of the current Sniffy file.
- To run (execute) a classical conditioning experiment that you have designed, select the **Run Classical Conditioning Experiment** command from the Experiment menu.
- Once the Run Classical Conditioning Experiment command has been executed, the Sniffy Lite program will run the experiment. *Be sure that the experiment is designed the way you want it before you execute the Run Classical Conditioning Experiment command!*
- If you quit (exit) the program or open another Sniffy file after executing the Run Classical Conditioning Experiment command, you will be asked whether you want to save the file. If you save it, the program will begin running the classical conditioning experiment exactly where it left off when you open the file the next time.
- If you realize you have made a mistake in setting up a stage of the experiment that has not already started to execute, you can choose the Design Classical Conditioning Experiment command and change the unexecuted stage(s).

The Sensitivity & Fear Mind Window

Here is a picture of the Sensitivity & Fear mind window.

[Sensitivity & Fear mind window graph showing two columns: "Pain Sensitivity" with a tall bar reaching about mid-range, and "Fear" with a very short bar near 0. Y-axis labeled from "0" to "Max".]

- The window's blue background color tells you that this is a mind window, not a measure of Sniffy's behavior.
- The column labeled Pain Sensitivity depicts Sniffy's sensitivity to the shock US and predicts the strength of his UR the next time the US occurs. In Sniffy Lite, Sniffy's shock sensitivity never changes. No matter how often the shock has been presented, its presentation will interrupt Sniffy's bar pressing for about 2 minutes.
- The column labeled **Fear** shows the current intensity of Sniffy's fear. Remember that this is not a measure of Sniffy's behavior; it is a measure of an internal psychological process. However, the more intense Sniffy's fear, the less likely he is to press the bar.

The CS Response Strength Mind Window

The CS Response Strength mind window displays the strength of the light CS's capacity to elicit a bar-press suppressing CR as a function of trials. At the top of the next page is the CS Response Strength mind window as it would be displayed at the end of a one-stage experiment in which the light CS was paired with the shock US 10 times.

Note the following features of this CS Response Strength mind window:

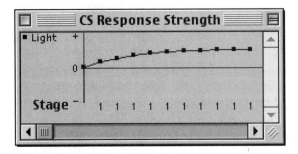

- The blue background color denotes that CS Response Strength window is a mind window, not a measure of Sniffy's behavior. The psychological state depicted is strength of the light CS's capacity to elicit a CR at the end of each trial. CS Response Strength predicts how strongly Sniffy will respond to a light the next time it is presented.
- The vertical axis of the graph indicates whether the CS Response Strength is excitatory or inhibitory. If a CS has an excitatory, positive tendency to elicit a bar-press-suppressing CR, its response strength will be greater than zero. If a CS had an inhibitory, negative tendency to prevent the occurrence of a CR, its response strength would be less than zero. In Sniffy Lite, the light's CS Response Strength will always be greater than or equal to zero.
- Beneath the horizontal axis of the graph to the right of the words **Stage** is a row of numerals. The numerals denote the stage of the experiment in which each trial occurs. In this example, the row of numerals consists of ten 1's because Stage 1 consisted of 10 trials and was the only stage in the experiment.

The Suppression-Ratio Window

Here is the Suppression Ratio window for the same experiment.

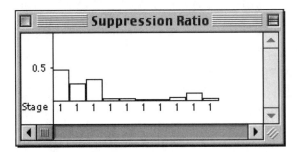

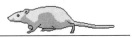

- The white background of this window indicates that it contains a measure of Sniffy's behavior.
- At the bottom of the graph, the row of numerals that appears to the right of the word "Stage" denotes the stages of the experiment. Because this experiment had only one stage, we see a row of ten 1's.
- The suppression ratio is about 0.5 on the first trial. After Trial 1, the suppression ratio decreases and then levels out at or just above 0 for the remainder of the experiment. Thus, the light CS acquired the capacity to elicit a strong CER.

The Cumulative Record During Classical Conditioning

Here is a fragment of Sniffy's cumulative record from the same experiment. Shown are three Stage 1 trials.

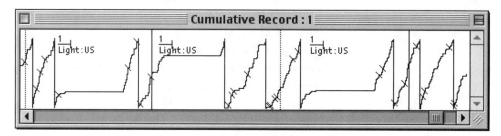

- The horizontal bars above instances of the word "Light" mark the durations of the CS. The notations of 1 indicate that these trials occurred during Stage 1. The word "Light" indicates that the light CS was presented, and the term US after the colon indicates that the light was paired with the shock US.
- Note how Sniffy stopped pressing the bar soon after the CS came on and that he did not start pressing the bar again for some time after the CS terminated. The cessation of bar pressing when the CS comes on is Sniffy's CR to the CS. The delay in his return to bar pressing after the CS terminates reflects Sniffy's UR to the shock US.

How to Get Reliable, Comparable Results

The CER is measured by observing changes in Sniffy's bar-pressing performance. The Sniffy Lite program computes the suppression ratio by comparing the number of times that Sniffy presses the bar during the 30-second CS with the number of times he presses it during the 30-second period just before the CS was presented. To make this measurement reliable, you want Sniffy to press the bar at a rapid, steady rate unless his response rate is being reduced because he is showing either a CR or UR. If Sniffy is not pressing the bar at a steady rate, you will obtain erratic results because the value of the suppression ratio is affected by the number of bar presses Sniffy makes during the 30 seconds prior to each CS presentation.

Variable-ratio (VR) schedules produce rapid, steady bar-press performances that make ideal baselines against which to measure suppression ratios. Thus we strongly recommend that you use a VR-trained Sniffy as the starting point for all your classical conditioning experiments. In fact, the surest way to get predictable results is to use the same baseline Sniffy file as the starting point for all your classical conditioning experiments. The baseline we used for calibrating the Sniffy Lite program is the VR25 file located in the Sample Files folder on your Sniffy Lite CD. We recommend you copy that file to your hard disk and use it as your classical conditioning baseline unless you have an explicit reason to use another baseline.

Your setting for the average Interval Between Trials can also affect the reliability of suppression-ratio measurements. As noted above, the Sniffy Lite program computes the suppression ratio on each trial by comparing Sniffy's response rate during the 30-second interval before the CS occurs with the response rate during the CS. Thus, to get a good suppression-ratio measurement, Sniffy needs to be pressing the bar throughout the 30-second period before the CS comes on. The default value for the average Interval Between Trials is 5 minutes. This setting is almost always long enough to ensure that Sniffy will be pressing away during the crucial 30-second interval before each CS presentation. If you shorten the Interval Between Trials to less than 5 minutes, you may encounter problems.

Putting Everything Together to Understand Classical Conditioning

During a classical conditioning experiment, you can observe four things:

- *Occurrences of the CS and US.*
- *Changes in Sniffy's psychological states.* These changes are visible in the Sensitivity & Fear and the CS Response Strength mind windows.

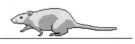

- *Sniffy's responses to the CS and US,* and especially how his response to the CS changes as a function of experience. You can observe Sniffy's responses to these stimuli by simply watching Sniffy's behavior during and after their presentation.
- *Response measures.* The Cumulative Record contains raw data about Sniffy's bar-pressing behavior throughout the experiment, shows when the different stimuli occur, and enables you to view the ways in which the stimuli affect Sniffy's bar pressing. The Suppression Ratio window contains the classical conditioning response measure that psychologists typically employ in CER experiments.
- Being able to see how stimulus events produce psychological changes that in turn produce behavior changes that in turn are reflected in behavioral measurements should enable you to develop a thorough understanding of the way in which psychologists believe classical conditioning works.

Exporting Your Results to Other Programs

During a classical conditioning experiment, the Sniffy Lite program enters data into the Suppression Ratio window and the CS Response Strength window. These graphs are saved as part of the Sniffy Lite file so that you can go back and examine your results after an experiment has been completed.

You can also export suppression ratio and CS response strength results to a spreadsheet or statistical analysis program where you can perform additional data analyses or produce more sophisticated graphs. To export the numeric data on which both the CS Response Strength and Suppression Ratio graphs are based:

- Click your (left) mouse button once while pointing the cursor at CS Response Strength window.
- Choose the Export Data command from the File menu. Executing the Export Data command will bring up the standard dialogue box for creating and saving a new file.
- Choose an appropriate name and select an appropriate place to save your data-export file on your computer's hard disk.
- The Export Data command creates a tab-delimited data file that you can then open while running most spreadsheet and statistical analysis programs.

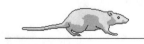

- To view the file in a spreadsheet or statistical analysis program,
  - □ Start the program in which you wish to view your exported Sniffy Lite data.
  - □ Choose the Open command from that program's file menu.
  - □ In the dialogue box that appears, go to the location on your hard drive where you saved the Sniffy Lite data-export file.
  - □ If the Sniffy Lite data-export file is not visible, choose the Show All Files option in the file-opening dialogue box.
  - □ If no Show All Files option is available or if the program does not open the file successfully when you select it, check to see whether the program has a special data-import command. If necessary, read your spreadsheet or statistical analysis program's manual or search its on-line help files to determine how to import a tab-delimited text file.

The next illustration shows some exported Sniffy Lite data as it appears in a typical spreadsheet program. In the experiment depicted, the light CS was paired with the shock US during 10 classical conditioning trials.

	A	B	C	D	E
1	Stage	S/R	Light	During CS	Pre-CS
2	1	0.4727	0.3	26	29
3	1	0.3333	0.5055	19	38
4	1	0.1206	0.6462	7	51
5	1	0.0731	0.7426	3	38
6	1	0.1162	0.8087	5	38
7	1	0.0909	0.8539	3	30
8	1	0.0833	0.8849	3	33
9	1	0.0526	0.9062	2	36
10	1	0.0606	0.9207	2	31
11	1	0.0425	0.9307	2	45

- The numerals under **Stage** show the number of the experimental stage for each trial. Because the experiment contained only one stage, the numeral 1 appears for each trial.
- The data under **S/R** are the numeric values of the suppression ratio for each trial.
- The data under **Light** are the CS Response Strength values for the Light CS at the end of each trial.
- The columns headed **During CS** and **Pre-CS** show the number of times that Sniffy pressed the bar during the CS and during the 30-second period immediately before the CS was presented.

Time-Saving Hints

Some of Sniffy's classical conditioning exercises require a considerable amount of time to run. Here are a couple of tips about how to perform them as quickly and as efficiently as possible:

- If your computer has enough random-access memory (RAM), you can set up a Sniffy exercise and let the program run the experiment in the background while you do something else on your computer. The program will run more slowly in the background than in the foreground, but that speed difference may be offset by the convenience of being able to do other necessary work while the program is performing an experiment.
- You can use the Isolate Sniffy (Accelerate Time) command to speed up execution of your classical conditioning experiments, but do so cautiously. Because the last two exercises involve adding additional stages to a previous exercise, you need to be careful to stop the program shortly after each exercise is completed. If you are using the time acceleration feature on a fast computer, it is easy to slip up and let the computer fill all 10 cumulative records that the program is capable of recording with unneeded data about Sniffy's performance on a VR schedule, after which you cannot add any additional stages to that particular Sniffy Lite file. The Sniffy Lite program includes two useful features to help you avoid this problem:
  - The program signals the end of a classical conditioning experiment by beeping at the end of the last currently programmed classical conditioning trial. When you hear that sound, wait (if necessary) until Sniffy has started to press the bar again. Then save the file and either quit (exit) the program or set up the next exercise you want to perform.
  - The Lab Assistant informs you about the status of your experiment. When a classical conditioning experiment is in progress, the Lab Assistant window provides several kinds of self-explanatory information about what is going on. When the classical conditioning experiment is complete, the Lab Assistant states, "You have chosen to reinforce Sniffy on a schedule." Thus, if you leave the room while your computer is running a classical conditioning experiment, a glance at the Lab Assistant window will tell you whether or not your classical conditioning experiment is complete.

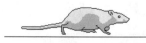

Exercise 14. Basic Acquisition

Acquisition is produced by setting up a series of trials in which a CS regularly precedes occurrences of the US. The following steps describe how to set up and run an experiment in which Sniffy receives 10 pairings of the light CS with the shock US.

1. Open a Sniffy Lite file in which Sniffy has been fully trained to bar press on a VR schedule. *We recommend you copy the file called VR25 that is located in the Sample Files folder on your Sniffy Lite CD to your hard disk and use it as the baseline file for this experiment.*

2. Use the Save As command in the File menu to save the file under an appropriate new name (such as Ex14-classacq) on your computer's hard drive.

3. Choose the Design Classical Conditioning Experiment command from the Experiment menu. In the Classical Conditioning Experimental Design dialogue box, make the following settings:

   a. In the Stage section, type 5 in the text box located to the right of Interval Between Trials to indicate that the average interval between trials will be 5 minutes.

   b. In the text box located to the right of Number of Trials, type 10.

   c. In the Second Stimulus panel of the dialogue box, select the shock US.

   d. Carefully check to see that you have selected the correct settings.

   e. Click the command button labeled Save.

4. After the Experimental Design Dialogue box has closed, choose the Run Classical Conditioning Experiment command from the Experiment menu.

5. If you want to speed up execution of the experiment, select the Isolate Sniffy (Accelerate Time) command from the Experiment menu. However, if you use this feature, be careful not to let the program run very long after the experiment is completed. The file this exercise creates is the basis for the next two exercises. Thus you want to avoid inadvertently filling cumulative records with unneeded VR-performance data once

> the classical conditioning experiment is finished. Remember that the program beeps at the end of a classical conditioning experiment. When you hear that sound, wait until Sniffy resumes bar pressing. Then save the file and quit (exit) the program.
>
> 6. After the last acquisition trial, save your results by selecting the save command from the File menu.

During the next 50 minutes of program time, the program will automatically run the experiment. While the program is running, the Suppression Ratio window will draw a bar graph that shows Sniffy's suppression ratio as a function of trials. At the same time, the CS Response Strength mind window will produce a line graph depicting changes in the CS's capacity to elicit a CR.

At the end of the experiment, your Suppression Ratio and CS Response Strength windows should resemble the following.

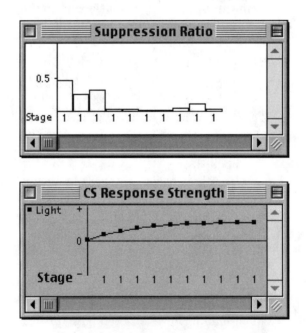

During acquisition, the suppression ratio starts out at around 0.5 on the first trial, then declines and levels off at an average value a little above zero. This decrease in the suppression ratio means that the tone CS is acquiring the capacity to suppress Sniffy's bar pressing. You can verify this fact by examining the cumulative record. During the last

several trials, Sniffy stops pressing the bar very quickly after the tone comes on. While the suppression ratio is decreasing, the CS Response Strength mind window shows that the tone's capacity to elicit a fear response is increasing. Remember that the Suppression Ratio window depicts a change in Sniffy's behavior, whereas the CS Response Strength mind window depicts the change in Sniffy's psychological state that causes the behavior change.

With a real rat, the animal's changing response to the CS would be the only thing you could observe. Many psychologists explain this behavior change by postulating that it results from a change in an unobservable psychological process. With the conditioned emotional response, the acquired capacity of a CS to elicit suppression of bar pressing is thought to be the result of an increasingly intense fear response. During CS presentations, the Sensitivity & Fear mind window displays the strength of Sniffy's fear; and the CS Response Strength mind window shows how strong the fear response will be when the CS is presented the next time. With Sniffy Lite, you can observe both the behavior change and the change in the Sniffy Lite program's classical conditioning algorithm that causes Sniffy's behavior to change. We have designed Sniffy's classical conditioning algorithm to resemble theoretical processes that psychologists (such as Guthrie, 1960; Hull, 1943, 1952; Rescorla & Wagner, 1972) have postulated in an effort to explain classical conditioning. However, nobody has ever seen anything closely analogous to CS Response Strength in a rat's brain; and it's impossible, even in principle, to observe the psychological (mental) processes of real animals. We believe that the Sniffy Lite program's mind windows will help you understand psychological explanations of classical conditioning, but it's important to remember that they do not provide any ultimate insights into the workings of the "animal mind."

An interesting thing to note is that the suppression ratio measure of Sniffy's response to the CS is not a perfect reflection of Sniffy's fear response. As the CS Response Strength mind window shows, Sniffy's fear response is at an almost constant high level during the last several acquisition trials. Yet the value of Sniffy's suppression ratio fluctuates somewhat from trial to trial. The suppression ratio varies because Sniffy's behavior is determined by a complex set of probabilities.

This variation in Sniffy's suppression ratio is somewhat analogous to the results that you obtain if you repeatedly perform an experiment in which you toss a coin 10 times. On any given coin toss, the probability that the coin will come up heads is equal to the probability that it will come up tails. For this reason, if you perform a great many 10-toss

experiments, the average number of heads will be 5. However, the exact number of heads will vary from experiment to experiment. Sometimes you will get 5 heads, sometimes 7 heads, sometimes 4 heads. The operation of similar processes accounts for the variation that you see in Sniffy's suppression ratio values. The suppression ratio is computed by comparing the number of times Sniffy presses the bar during the 30-second period preceding each CS presentation with the number of bar presses during each 30-second CS presentation. The computed suppression ratios vary because Sniffy's response rates vary during both periods. The suppression ratios that psychologists obtain with real animals vary in a similar fashion, and probably for similar reasons.

Exercise 15. Extinction

These instructions assume you have already run the acquisition experiment just described. To set up a series of 30 extinction trials, you should follow the steps listed. You need to give more extinction than acquisition trials because the CER extinguishes much more slowly than it is acquired.

1. Start the Sniffy Lite program and open the file we suggested you call Ex14-classacq, in which Sniffy acquired a CR to the light CS.
2. Use the Save As command to save the file under a new name (for example, Ex15-classext) on your computer's hard drive. Saving the file under a new name preserves the original file in which Sniffy has been classically conditioned for future use.
3. Choose the Design Classical Conditioning Experiment command from the Experiment menu. The Classical Conditioning Experimental Design dialogue box opens to Stage 1. All the options for defining conditions are dimmed because Stage 1 has already been run.
4. In the Design Classical Conditioning Experiment dialogue box, make the following settings to define Stage 2, which will contain your extinction trials:
   a. Click on the command button labeled New Stage. The number after View/Edit Experimental Stage changes from 1 to 2 to indicate that you are now working on Stage 2 of the ex-

periment. Because this is a new stage that has not yet been run, all the options for defining trial types are available.

b. Be sure that the numeral 5 appears in the text box after Interval Between Trials.

c. Type 30 in the text box located to the right of Number of Trials.

d. In the Second Stimulus panel, choose None.

e. Carefully check your settings.

f. Click on the Save button at the bottom of the dialogue box to save the experimental design.

5. After the Classical Conditioning Experimental Design dialogue box closes, choose the Run Classical Conditioning Experiment command from the Experiment menu.

6. If you want to speed up the experiment, select the Isolate Sniffy (Accelerate Time) command from the Experiment menu. Because you will need to use the file from this exercise as the starting point for the next exercise, avoid inadvertently filling up cumulative records by letting the program run for very long after this exercise is complete.

7. When the program has finished running the experiment, choose the Save command from the File menu to save your results.

During the next 150 minutes of program time, the Sniffy Lite program will automatically give Sniffy 30 extinction trials—that is, 30 trials during which the CS occurs without the US. As the program executes, the Sniffy Lite program will draw a graph showing Sniffy's suppression ratio on each trial in the Suppression Ratio window and the strength of Sniffy's fear response on each trial in the CS Response Strength window. At the end of extinction, your Suppression Ratio and CS Response Strength windows should resemble the following.

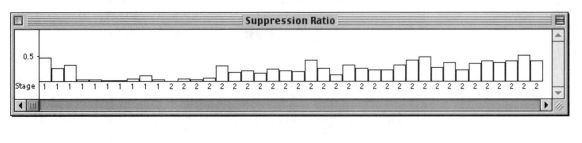

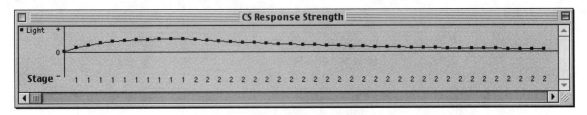

The Suppression Ratio window shows that repeatedly presenting the CS without the US causes the CS to gradually stop eliciting suppression of Sniffy's bar pressing. The CS Response Strength mind window shows that this behavior change is the result of the CS's losing its capacity to elicit a fear response. Once again note the variability in the suppression ratio that reflects the probabilistic nature Sniffy's behavior.

Exercise 16. Spontaneous Recovery

Here are the steps that you need to follow to observe spontaneous recovery.

1. Open the file we suggested you call Ex15-classext from Exercise 15 in which Sniffy was first conditioned in Stage 1 and then extinguished in Stage 2.
2. Use the Save As command to save the file under an appropriate new name (such as Ex16-ClassSponRec) on your computer's hard drive.
3. Under the Experiment menu, choose Remove Sniffy for Time-Out. This operation simulates removing Sniffy from the operant chamber, leaving him in his home cage for 24 hours, and then returning him to the experimental situation.
4. Choose Design Classical Conditioning Experiment from the Experiment menu and make the following settings in the Classical Conditioning Experimental Design dialogue box to give Sniffy a second 10-trial extinction session:
   a. The dialogue box opens (as always) to Stage 1. All alternatives for defining trials and stimuli are dimmed because Stage 1 has already been run.
   b. To define a new Stage 3, you must first move to Stage 2 because new stages are always inserted immediately after the stage currently being displayed. In the Stage section of the

dialogue box, click on Next Stage to move to Stage 2, which has also already been run.

c. When you reach Stage 2, click on New Stage to create the new Stage 3 after Stage 2. Note that the numeral 3 is now present after View/Edit Experiment Stage.

d. Be sure that the Interval Between Trials at 5 minutes.

e. Set Number of Trials to 10.

f. In the Second Stimulus panel, choose None.

g. Carefully check your settings.

h. Click on the Save command button at the bottom of the dialogue box to save the experimental design.

5. After the dialogue box closes, choose the Run Classical Conditioning Experiment command from the Experiment menu.

6. If you want to speed up the experiment, select the Isolate Sniffy (Accelerate Time) command from the Experiment menu.

7. When the experiment has finished running, save the file.

As Stage 3 executes, the suppression ratio will be graphed as a function of trials in the Suppression Ratio window and the strength of Sniffy's fear response will be graphed in the CS Response Strength mind window as follows.

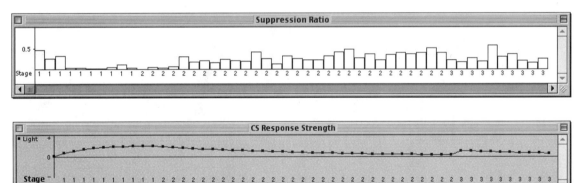

Early in Stage 3, Sniffy's average suppression ratio is somewhat lower than the average suppression ratio at the end of Stage 2, and his CS Response Strength is somewhat higher. As the second extinction session proceeds, the average suppression ratios goes back up; and the CS Response Strength drops back toward zero.

APPENDIX 1 User's Guide to Commands and Dialogue Boxes

This section provides a quick overview of the menu commands available in Sniffy Lite. A full description of Sniffy Lite windows is available in the Sniffy Tutor. The Sniffy Tutor also contains a brief discussion of the program's principal commands. The Sniffy Tutor illustrates the most common procedures required to save and open Sniffy data files, as well as the menu commands required to set up training and testing scenarios.

The File Menu

The File menu contains the standard operating-system commands for saving and opening files: **New**, **Open**, **Save**, **Save As**, **Revert**, **Print**, and **Exit (Quit)**. See the Appendix 2 if you need detailed information about how to save and open files.

- **New** provides a new rat ready to be trained.
- **Revert** restores the file to the state it was in the last time you saved it.
- **Close** dismisses the currently active window. (To display the window again, select it from the Windows menu.)
- **Export Data** produces a tab-delimited text file containing the data in the currently active window. These data files can be opened in most spreadsheet and statistical analysis programs. You can use this command with the Cumulative Record, Suppression Ratio, and CS Response Strength windows.
- **Print Window** prints the currently active window. You can use this command with any window except the Operant Chamber.

■ **Preferences** brings up the following dialogue box.

> **Configuration Preferences**
>
> ┌─ **Environment Parameters** ─────────────────────
> │ ☑ **Animate Sniffy**   Slow   ○ ○ ● ○ ○ Fast
> │ ☑ **Limit Colors to :**   Few   ○ ○ ● ○ ○ Lots
> │ ☑ **Sound Proof Cage**
> └──
>
> [**Use Defaults**]   [Cancel] [**OK**]

In the dialogue box,

- ❑ The **Animate Sniffy** settings control Sniffy's animation.
  - ❑ The Slow–Fast settings determine the speed of Sniffy's movements when he is visible in the operant chamber.
  - ❑ Placing a checkmark next to Animate Sniffy causes Sniffy to be visible.
  - ❑ Clicking on the box next to Animate Sniffy to remove the checkmark is equivalent to executing the Isolate Sniffy (Accelerate Time) command, which is explained later under the description of commands for the Experiment menu.
- ❑ **Limit Colors to:** enables Macintosh users to control the number of colors displayed in the Sniffy Lite program. The number of colors displayed in other programs is unaffected. This setting is unavailable to Windows users. In Windows, the number of colors displayed is determined by a setting in the Display section of the Control Panel; and this setting affects the display of colors in all programs.
- ❑ **Sound Proof Cage**, when selected, turns off the program's sound effects. (Selecting this option will make you more popular with your roommates or family!)

The Edit Menu

Edit	Experiment	Windows
Undo
Cut
Copy
Copy Window Image
Paste
Clear

■ The **Undo**, **Copy**, **Cut**, **Paste**, and **Clear** commands are not implemented in this version of Sniffy Lite.

■ **Copy Window Image** copies a bitmap image of the contents of the currently active window to the clipboard. This command provides a convenient way to insert images from Sniffy Lite windows in a word

processor document. To insert an image from a Sniffy Lite window into a word processor document:

☐ Select the window whose image you want to copy by clicking on the window once with your (left) mouse button.

☐ Execute the Copy Window Image command.

☐ Go to the place in your word processor document where you want to insert the image. (If your computer has enough RAM, you can run your word processor and Sniffy Lite at the same time.)

☐ Select the Paste (or Paste Special) command from the File menu of the word processor program to insert your Sniffy Lite image into the word processor document.

The Experiment Menu

Experiment	Windows	Help
Design Operant Experiment...		
Remove Sniffy for Time-Out		
Design Classical Conditioning Experiment...		
Run Classical Conditioning Experiment		
Isolate Sniffy (Accelerated Time)		

The commands in the Experiment menu determine the experimental conditions that are in effect during operant and classical conditioning experiments.

Design Operant Experiment

Selecting Design Operant Experiment brings up the following dialogue box, which is used to control operant-conditioning experiments.

Design Operant Experiment

Reinforcement Schedule

○ Fixed   ○ Seconds
○ Variable   ● Responses
● Continuous

○ Extinction   ☑ Mute Pellet Dispenser

Cancel   OK

- This dialogue box determines conditions of reinforcement.
- Selecting **Continuous** causes each bar press to be reinforced. This is the default condition in effect whenever you create a new Sniffy file by executing the New command under the File menu.
- To set up a schedule of reinforcement:
  - ☐ Select **Fixed** for fixed-interval (FI) or fixed-ratio (FR) schedules.
  - ☐ Select **Variable** for variable-interval (VI) or variable-ratio (VR) schedules.
  - ☐ Select **Responses** for ratio (FR or VR) schedules.
  - ☐ Select **Seconds** for interval (FI or VI) schedules.
  - ☐ The numeral that you type in the text box in this section determines the value of the schedule in responses for ratio schedules or seconds for interval schedules.
- Selecting **Extinction** causes reinforcement to be turned off. None of Sniffy's bar presses produce food pellets.
  - ☐ Selecting **Mute Pellet Dispenser** eliminates the sound of the pellet dispenser as a consequence of bar pressing. To produce **standard extinction** conditions, this option should be turned on.
  - ☐ If Mute Pellet Dispenser is not selected, Sniffy will continue to hear the sound of the pellet dispenser when he presses the bar. Extinction with Mute Pellet Dispenser turned off is employed to study the effect of **secondary reinforcement**.

Remove Sniffy for Time-Out

Executing the Remove Sniffy for Time-Out command brings up the following dialogue box.

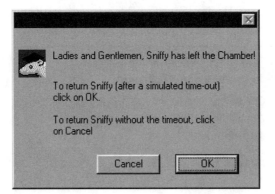

- This command is used in experiments on **spontaneous recovery**.

- See Chapters 3 and 5 for detailed descriptions of experiments in which the command is employed.
- In the dialogue box,
  - Clicking the OK command button simulates giving Sniffy a 24-hour rest period in his home cage.
  - Clicking the Cancel command button dismisses the dialogue box without giving Sniffy a rest period.

Design Classical Conditioning Experiment

Executing the Design Classical Conditioning Experiment command brings up the following dialogue box. Settings in this dialogue box determine the experimental conditions in effect during classical conditioning experiments. Detailed instructions for using this dialogue box are given in Chapter 6.

Run Classical Conditioning Experiment

Executing the Run Classical Conditioning Experiment command causes the Sniffy Lite program to execute a classical conditioning experiment that has been saved in the Design Classical Conditioning Experiment dialogue box. The command is dimmed (unavailable) if no classical conditioning experimental design has been specified or if a classical conditioning experiment is in progress.

Isolate Sniffy (Accelerate Time)

- The Isolate Sniffy (Accelerate Time) command is available whenever Sniffy is visible.
- Executing the command replaces the view of Sniffy moving around in his operant chamber with the following graphic.

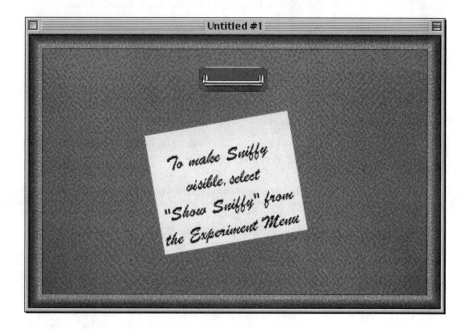

- The graphic depicts the outside of a sound-proof, air-conditioned chamber of the type that many psychologists who study operant conditioning employ to isolate their easily distracted live animals from extraneous stimuli in the laboratory
- Whenever this graphic is visible, your computer will run the current experiment much faster than when Sniffy is visible because the computer does not have to display Sniffy's movements.

Show Sniffy

- The Show Sniffy command is available whenever Sniffy's isolation chamber is being displayed.
- Executing the command causes the Sniffy animation to reappear.

The Windows Menu

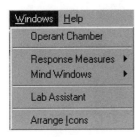

The commands in the Windows menu make specific Sniffy Lite windows visible. Selecting a window will reopen a window that has been closed or bring to the front any window that is currently obscured by another window. Note that the **response measures** and the **mind windows** are grouped in separate submenus.

APPENDIX 2
How to Manage Your Sniffy Lite Files

Floppy Disks and Hard Disks

Floppy disks are small, portable devices that can hold small amounts of data. The picture here shows a floppy disk of the kind used in contemporary Windows and Macintosh computers. Each floppy disk is capable of storing about 1400 kilobytes (KB) of data.

In addition, your computer contains one or more hard disks. A **hard disk** is a device located inside your computer. The hard disks in contemporary computers usually have storage capacities ranging from as little as 800 megabytes (MB) up to 10 gigabytes (GB) of data. The fact that 1 MB = 1024 KB, and 1 GB = 1024 MB means that your computer's hard disk can store from several hundred to over a thousand times as much data as a floppy disk.

Sniffy Lite data files range in size from as little as 160 KB for the shortest, least complex exercises up to about 500 KB for the longest, most complex exercises. The point of all this arithmetic is to point out that, although you cannot store very many Sniffy files on a floppy disk, you can store a great many of them on your computer's hard disk. This fact is why *we strongly urge you to save your Sniffy files on your computer's hard disk.*

In addition, Sniffy data files grow during experiments. A Sniffy file that occupies 200 KB of disk space when you save it immediately after setting up an experiment might require 400–500 KB of disk space when you save it again after the experiment has been completed. Sniffy files grow as experiments progress because the Sniffy Lite program records a lot of information about Sniffy's behavior and psychological processes during experiments. For this reason, if you didn't follow our advice and saved a Sniffy file on a floppy disk, the floppy disk might have enough room to save the file at the beginning of the experiment but not at the

91

end. In that event, you would get an error message when you tried to save the file on the floppy disk at the end of the experiment; and you might end up having to do the exercise over again. This is another reason why *we implore you to save your Sniffy files on your hard disk, not on a floppy disk.*

Here are some tips that will save time and minimize frustration.

- *Always save your Sniffy files on the hard disk of the computer you're using.*
- If your professor wants you to hand in your Sniffy files on a floppy disk:
  - Save the files on the hard disk of the computer that you're using when you create the files.
  - Then copy the files from the computer's hard disk onto one or more floppy disks and give them to your professor when the time comes to hand in the files. We explain in detail how to copy files onto floppy disks in a later section of this appendix.
  - A second advantage of this approach is that if you (or your professor) loses the floppy disk containing your precious files, you will still have a copy of the files on your computer's hard disk.
- *If you don't have your own computer* and must store your Sniffy files on floppy disks:
  - Save your Sniffy files on the hard disk of the computer you're using when you create the files.
  - When the experiment is completed, copy your files from the hard disk onto one or more floppy disks.
  - Before you use the files again, copy your files from your floppy disks back onto the hard disk of the computer you're using.
  - Because floppy disks are fragile and easy to damage, always keep at least two copies of your files on different floppy disks.
- *Here are some tips to reduce the chance of losing data stored on floppy disks:*
  - Keep your floppy disks in a sturdy container designed for storing floppy disks.
  - Never carry an unprotected floppy disk in your pocket or purse.
  - Keep your floppy disks away from heat sources such as radiators or hot sunlight.
  - Keep your floppy disks away from anything that contains a magnet. For example, don't set a floppy disk down on top of a stereo speaker, which contains a magnet that could erase the data. Telephone hand sets also contain magnets that may be a hazard to floppy disks.

Deciding Where to Save Your Files

Unless you specify other settings, the Sniffy Lite Installer places the Sniffy Lite program, Sniffy Tutor, Sample Files, and a Read Me file in predictable places on your computer's hard disk.

In Windows, the installer places these items in a folder called Sniffy Lite for Windows, which is located inside a folder called Program Files, which is on your C drive. The following picture shows a typical Windows installation.

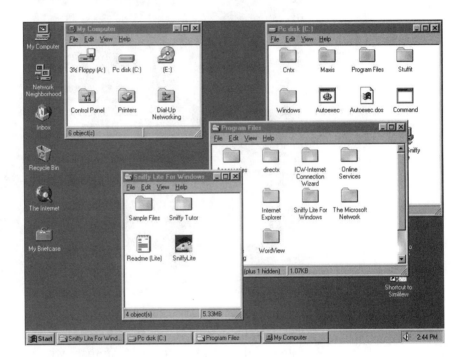

The open Sniffy Lite for Windows folder is displayed in front of the open Program Files folder, which is in front of the open Pc disk [C:] window. We also see the open My Computer window. To display the windows like this, you would do the following:

- Double-click with your left mouse button while pointing at the My Computer icon. Unless you've moved it, the My Computer icon will be in the upper left-hand corner of your Windows desktop.
- In the My Computer window, double-click with your left mouse button while pointing at the Pc disk [C] icon.

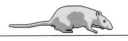

- In the Pc disk [C] window, double-click with your left mouse button while pointing at the Program Files folder.
- In the Program Files window, double-click with your left mouse button while pointing at the Sniffy Lite for Windows folder.
- Rearrange and resize the windows to display them as shown.

The next picture shows a typical Macintosh installation.

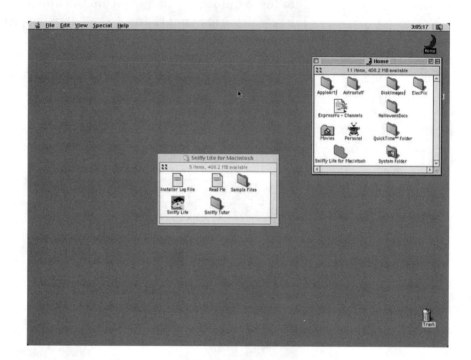

The installer places the Sniffy Lite program and other material inside a folder called Sniffy Lite for Macintosh, which is located on your startup disk. We see the open Sniffy Lite for Macintosh folder next to the window showing all the folders that are visible when the root-level window for a hard disk called Home is opened. To display the windows like this:

- Double-click the mouse button while pointing the cursor at the icon of the startup disk. The startup disk icon is always located in the upper right-hand corner of your desktop.
- Inside the open startup disk window, double-click the mouse button while pointing the cursor at the Sniffy Lite for Macintosh folder.
- Rearrange and resize the windows to display them as shown.

So that you know where to find them, you should store all your Sniffy Lite files in the same place on your hard disk. Inside your Sniffy Lite for Windows or Sniffy Lite for Macintosh folder would be one logical place to keep your Sniffy Lite files. Alternatively, if you like to be neat, you might want to create a new folder called My Sniffy Files inside your Sniffy Lite for Windows or Sniffy Lite for Macintosh folder and keep your Sniffy files there.

To create a new folder in Windows:

- Point the cursor at the File menu located at the top of your Sniffy Lite for Windows folder window and click your left mouse button.
- In the drop-down menu that appears, drag down to New, then drag across to Folder, and release the mouse button. A new folder appears.
- Immediately type the name that you want to give the new folder.

To create a new folder on a Macintosh:

- Click your mouse button once while pointing at your open Sniffy Lite for Macintosh folder window. (This operation ensures that the new folder will be created in the right window).
- Choose the New Folder command from the Finder's File menu. A new untitled folder appears.
- Immediately type the name that you want to give the folder.

Getting Easy Access to the Sniffy Lite Program and Your Sniffy Lite Files from Your Computer Desktop

Creating a Windows Shortcut

The ordinary way of reaching your Sniffy Lite for Windows folder involves the following steps:

- Open My Computer by double-clicking on its desktop icon with your left mouse button.
- Open Pc disk [C:] by double-clicking on its icon in the My Computer window.
- Open the Program Files folder in the Pc disk [C] window.
- Open the Sniffy Lite for Windows folder inside the Program Files window.

What a process! Fortunately, there is a simple way to reduce the number of steps involved: Create a shortcut to your Sniffy Lite for Windows folder and place the shortcut on your Windows desktop. Here is what you need to do to set up the shortcut:

- Go through the first three steps just listed to open your Program Files window.
- While pointing the cursor at the Sniffy Lite for Windows folder icon, click and hold down your right mouse button.
- A drop-down menu appears with a number of commands listed.
- Release the mouse button, drag the cursor down to the Create Shortcut command, and click the mouse button again.
- A folder icon with an arrow on it entitled Shortcut to Sniffy Lite for Windows appears inside your Program Files folder.
- Click on the shortcut icon with your left mouse button, hold the mouse button down, and drag the icon onto your Windows desktop.
- Once the shortcut icon is on the desktop, you can drag it around to place it wherever you want it.
- In the future, all you have to do to open your Sniffy Lite for Windows folder is to double-click the shortcut with your left mouse button.

If you want to, you can also create and place shortcuts to the Sniffy Lite program and to your My Sniffy Files folder on your desktop.

Creating a Macintosh Alias

The ordinary way of getting to your Sniffy Lite for Macintosh folder involves the following steps:

- Double-click on the icon of your Macintosh hard-disk icon, which is located in the upper right-hand corner of your desktop, to open the hard-disk root window.
- Double-click on the Sniffy Lite for Macintosh folder icon to open the folder window.

Although this process is not as laborious as the analogous operation in Windows, it still might be handy to be able to access your Sniffy Lite for Macintosh folder directly from your desktop. To create that direct access, you need to create an alias of the Sniffy Lite for Macintosh folder and place the alias on your desktop. Here's what you need to do:

- Open the Macintosh hard-disk window by double-clicking on the hard-disk icon located in the upper right-hand corner of your desktop.
- Select the Sniffy Lite for Macintosh folder icon by clicking on it once.
- Select the Make Alias command from the File menu. A replica of the Sniffy Lite for Macintosh folder icon called *Sniffy Lite for Macintosh alias* appears in the hard-disk window. You can tell it's an alias two ways: The name says so, and the name is written in italics. Depending on what version of the system software you're using, a small arrow may also appear on the icon.
- To place the alias on your desktop, click on the alias icon, hold down your mouse button, and drag the icon onto the desktop.
- Once the alias is on the desktop, you can drag it around and place it wherever you want it.
- Double-clicking the alias icon opens your Sniffy Lite for Macintosh folder directly, without having to open the hard-disk window.

If you want to, you can also place aliases of the Sniffy Lite program and your My Sniffy Files folder on your desktop.

Saving Files

Let's imagine that you have come to the point in the instructions for an exercise where we tell you to execute the Save As command and save the exercise with some specified name in an appropriate place on your computer's hard disk. The following specific information tells Windows and Macintosh users what they need to do then to save their files in the place where they want to keep their Sniffy Lite files.

Saving Files in Windows

We assume you want to save a file in a folder called My Sniffy Files that is located inside the Sniffy Lite for Windows folder on your hard disk.

- Select the Save As command from the File menu in the Sniffy Lite program.

- A dialogue box resembling the following will appear.

Save As	? X
Save in: ⌷ Sniffy Lite For Windows ▼	⬆ 📁 ▤ ▦

My Sniffy Files
Sample Files
Sniffy Tutor

| File name: | | Save |
| Save as type: | Sniffy Data Files (*.SDF) ▼ | Cancel |

- Look carefully at the dialogue box.
- At the top after the words "Save in:" is a space containing an icon and the name of the place where the file will be saved unless you do something to change the location. In this case, the icon is a picture of an open folder, which tells you that the current place is a folder. Different icons would appear for different kinds of places (such as the desktop, a floppy disk, or the root level of a hard disk).[1]
- In the large white space below the place name are some closed folder icons with the names My Sniffy Files, Sample Files, and Sniffy Tutor. This part of the dialogue box always displays the contents of the place named in the area to the right of the "Save in:" label. Depending on what's in the currently displayed location, you may see names and icons representing files, folders, hard disks, or a floppy disk.
- If the name after "Save in:" is the right place where you want to save your file, all you have to do at this point is
  - ☐ In the text box located to the right of "File name:" type the name that you want to give the file.
  - ☐ Point the cursor at the Save command button and click once with your left mouse button.

[1]The root level of a hard disk is the contents that you see when you open a hard-disk icon by double-clicking on it.

- However, in this example the folder name after "Save in:" is Sniffy Lite for Windows, and we are assuming you want to save your file in the folder called My Sniffy Files. To do so, you would point the cursor at My Sniffy Files and double-click with your left mouse button. Doing that would move you to the My Sniffy Files folder as evidenced by the fact that the words My Sniffy Files now appear to the right of the words "Save in:" in the space at the top of the dialogue box.
- Now that you're in the right place, all you have to do is
  - □ Point the cursor at the text box to right of "File name:" and click the left mouse button once.
  - □ Type the name you want to give the file.
  - □ Point the cursor at the Save command button and click once with your left mouse button.
- On the right-hand side of the space at the top of the dialogue box where the current place name is displayed is a button with a triangle on it. Pointing the cursor at that button and clicking the left mouse button causes a drop-down menu to appear, as shown in the next picture.

Save As				? ☒
Save in:	Sniffy Lite For Windows ▼			
My Sniffy F	🖴 3½ Floppy (A:)		▲	
Sample Fil	🖴 Pc disk (C:)			
Sniffy Tutc	📁 Program Files			
	📁 Sniffy Lite For Windows			
	💿 (E:)			
	🖥 Network Neighborhood			
	💼 My Briefcase			
	📁 Online Services		▼	
File name:				Save
Save as type:	Sniffy Data Files (*.SDF) ▼			Cancel

- Moving the cursor up and down in this drop-down menu enables you to select other locations in which to save files. A scroll bar at the right-hand side of the drop-down menu enables you to display the entire list.

Saving Files on a Macintosh

We assume that you want to save a file in a folder called My Sniffy Files that is located inside the Sniffy Lite for Macintosh folder on your hard disk.

- Select the Save As command from the File menu in the Sniffy Lite program.
- A dialogue box resembling the following will appear.

```
┌─────────────────────────────────────────────────────────┐
│  ┌──────────────────────────────┐  ┌──┬──┬──┬──┐         │
│  │ 🗄 Sniffy Lite for Macintosh ⬍│  │🗄│⌷│🗐│🔍│         │
│  ├──────────────────────────────┤  └──┴──┴──┴──┘         │
│  │ ▦ Installer Log File      ▲  │  ┌───────────┐          │
│  │ 🗀 My Sniffy Files         ▓  │  │   Eject   │          │
│  │ ▦ Read Me                 ▓  │  └───────────┘          │
│  │ 🗀 Sample Files            ▓  │  ┌───────────┐          │
│  │ 🐟 Sniffy Lite            ▼  │  │  Desktop  │          │
│  │                              │  └───────────┘          │
│  │                              │  ┌───────────┐          │
│  │                              │  │  New 🗀   │          │
│  └──────────────────────────────┘  └───────────┘          │
│   Save File As:                    ┌───────────┐          │
│  ┌──────────────────────────────┐  │  Cancel   │          │
│  │ Untitled #1                  │  └───────────┘          │
│  └──────────────────────────────┘  ┌───────────┐          │
│                                    │   Save    │          │
│                                    └───────────┘          │
└─────────────────────────────────────────────────────────┘
```

Look carefully at the dialogue box.

- At the top, the panel that says Sniffy Lite for Macintosh tells you the name of the place where the file will be saved unless you do something to change the location.
- The icon just to the left of the place name tells you what kind of place it is. In this case, the folder icon tells you that it's a folder. Different icons would appear for the desktop, a floppy disk, or the root level of a hard disk.[2]
- The text box under "Save File As:" is where you type the name that you want to give the file. Because in this instance the file has not yet been named, the name "Untitled #1" appears.
  - □ The highlight color[3] in the text box tells you that the suggested name will be automatically replaced if you just start typing.

---

[2]The root level of a hard disk is the contents that you see when you open a hard-disk icon by double-clicking on it.

[3]You can select different highlight colors in a control panel. Depending on what version of the operating system you are using, the control panel in which you determine the highlight color may be called "Appearance" or "Colors."

□ If the background of the text box is white, you need to point the cursor at the text box and click your mouse button once before you start typing. If the wrong name is there, you also need to delete the old name before typing the new one. To delete the old name, drag across it while holding down the mouse button, then hit the Delete key on your keyboard.

- The large space in the middle of the dialogue box displays the alphabetized contents of the place named at the top. In this instance, we see that the folder named Sniffy Lite for Macintosh contains items called Installer Log, My Sniffy Files, Read Me, and so on. The icons to the left of the names tell you what kinds of items they are. Installer Log and Read Me are document files. My Sniffy Files is a folder. Sniffy Lite is a program. The icons that denote places where files could be saved appear in full color. The other icons are dimmed. The scroll bar on the right-hand side enables you to scroll up and down to see everything on the list.

- We are assuming you want to save your file in the folder called My Sniffy Files. To select that folder, point the cursor at it and double-click your mouse button. You know you have moved there when My Sniffy Files appears in the place name panel at the top of the dialogue box.

- Once you're in the place where you want to save your file,
  □ In the text box under "Save File As:" type the name that you want to give the file.
  □ Point the cursor at the Save command button and click your mouse button once.

- Clicking your mouse button once while pointing the cursor at the panel containing the name of the current place causes a drop-down menu to appear, as shown in the next picture.

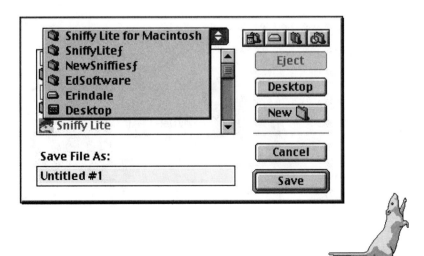

- Scrolling up and down in this drop-down menu enables you to move to other places where files can be saved.

Opening Files

Opening Files in Windows

There are several ways to open files in Windows, but we will describe only the most basic approach. We assume that you have already started the Sniffy Lite program and that you have just executed the Open command found under the File menu. When you execute the Open command, the Sniffy Lite program will always put up a dialogue box asking whether you want to save the file that is currently open. If you want to save the file, click on the Yes command button and go through the file-saving process. When the file has been saved, the following dialogue box will appear. If you do not want to save the file (for example, because you've just started the Sniffy Lite program and there is no point in saving an Untitled file that contains no data), click the No command button, and a dialogue box resembling the following will appear.

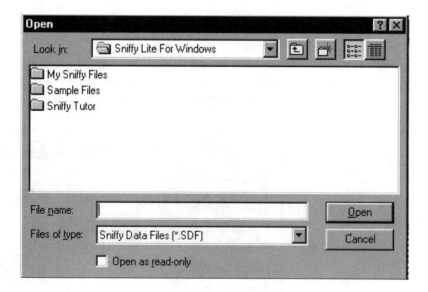

In many ways, the Open dialogue box resembles the Save dialogue box. Here are the main things to note about it:

- At the top in the space to the right of "Look in:" is the name of the place (the folder or disk) whose contents are currently being shown.
- The icon just to the left of the place name tells you what kind of place it is. In the example, the open-folder icon tells us we are examining the contents of a folder.
- At the right-hand side of the place name is a button with a triangle on it. Clicking on this button will produce a drop-down menu showing the current place in the hierarchy of folders and drives where there might be files you could open. If you need to, you can scroll around in this drop-down menu to find the file you want.
- In the large area in the middle of the dialogue box is a listing of the contents of place named at the top. You will see the names of the various items with icons that identify what kinds of items they are.
- When you see the name of the file you want to open, point the cursor at its name and click your left mouse button once. The name of the file will appear in the text box located to the right of "File name:" at the bottom of the dialogue box.
- If you've identified the right item, point the cursor at the Open command button and click your left mouse button once to open the file.

Opening Files on a Macintosh

There are several ways to open files on a Macintosh, but we will describe only the most basic approach. We assume that you have already started the Sniffy Lite program and that you have just executed the Open command found under the File menu. When you execute the Open command, the Sniffy Lite program will always put up a dialogue box asking whether you want to save the file that is currently open. If you want to save the file, click on the Save command button and go through the file-saving process. When the file has been saved, the following dialogue box will appear. If you do not want to save the file (for example, because you've just started the Sniffy Lite program and there is no point in saving an Untitled file that contains no data), click the Don't Save command button, and a dialogue box resembling that shown next will appear.

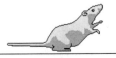

> **Choose an animal as the subject of this experiment.**
>
> 🖬 **Sniffy Lite for Macintosh** ⬍   🗄 📁 📑 🗃
>
> | 🖩 **Installer Log File** | ▲ | [**Eject**] |
> | 🗂 **My Sniffy Files** | | [**Desktop**] |
> | 🖩 **Read Me** | | |
> | 🗂 **Sample Files** | | [**Cancel**] |
> | 🗂 **Sniffy Tutor** | ▼ | [**Open**] |

In many ways, this Open dialogue box resembles the Save dialogue box. Here are the main things to note about it:

- At the top under "Choose an animal as the subject of this experiment" is a panel containing the name of the place (the folder or disk) whose contents are currently being shown.
- The icon just to the left of the place name tells you what kind of place it is. In the example, the folder icon tells us we are examining the contents of a folder.
- Clicking on the place name panel will produce a drop-down menu showing where in the hierarchy of folders and disks there might be files that you could open. If you need to, you can scroll around in this drop-down menu to find the place containing the file that you want.
- In the large area below the place name panel is a listing of the contents of the place named at the top of the dialogue box. You see the names of the various items with icons that identify what kinds of items they are. In the example, we see the names of two files and three folders.
- If you thought the file you wanted to open was in the My Sniffy Files folder, you would point the cursor at the name of that folder and double-click your mouse button. This action would open the My Sniffy Files folder as evidenced by the fact that the name of that folder would now appear in the place name panel at the top of the dialogue box.
- When you see the file you want to open, point the cursor at its name and click your mouse button once. As soon as you select the name of

a file that the Sniffy Lite program can open, the Open command button on the right-hand side of the dialogue box will be highlighted.

- Point the cursor at the highlighted Open command button and click your mouse button once to open the file.

Copying Files from a Hard Disk to a Floppy Disk

Instructions for Windows Users

- Place a floppy disk in your floppy-disk drive.
- Open My Computer by double-clicking the icon with that name on your Windows desktop. Unless you've moved it, the My Computer icon is in the upper left-hand corner of the desktop.
- Open the folder in which you keep your Sniffy Lite files. This will probably be either the folder entitled Sniffy Lite for Windows, which is inside the Program Files folder on your C drive or the folder that we suggested you call My Sniffy Files, which should be inside your Sniffy Lite for Windows folder.
- Inside the My Computer window is an icon called "3 1/2 Floppy [A:]".
- Arrange the My Computer window and the window containing the files that you want to copy so that both the names of the files and the 3 1/2 Floppy [A:] icon are visible.
- Use your left mouse button to select one or more files. You can select a single file by pointing the cursor at it and clicking. You can select several adjacent files by holding down the left mouse button and dragging across the file names and icons. You know when you have selected a file because it darkens.
- Point the cursor at the darkened area, hold down the left mouse button, and drag the file or files onto the 3 1/2 Floppy [A:] icon. When the icon darkens, release the mouse button. (As an alternative, you could open the 3 1/2 Floppy [A:] window and drag the files that you want to copy into the open floppy-disk window.)
- Windows will present an animation telling you that it is copying the files.
- If there is not enough room on the floppy disk to hold all the files you want to copy, Windows will put up a dialogue box saying that the destination disk is full. If that happens:
  □ Remove the full floppy disk from the floppy drive by pressing the button on the front of the drive.

    □ Insert a new floppy.

    □ Click on the Retry command button on the full-disk dialogue box to continue copying on the new floppy disk.

Instructions for Macintosh Users

- Insert a floppy disk in your floppy-disk drive.[4]
- The floppy-disk icon will appear on the right-hand side of your desktop in the first available space under the icon for your startup disk.
- Open the folder in which you have stored your Sniffy files on your hard disk.
- Place the folder window in a position so that both the names of the files that you want to copy and the floppy-disk icon are visible.
- Use your mouse button to select one or more files. You can select a single file by pointing the cursor at it and clicking. Or you can select several adjacent files by holding down the mouse button and dragging across the file names and icons. You know when you have selected a file because it darkens.
- Point the cursor at the darkened area, hold down the mouse button, and drag the files onto the floppy-disk icon. When the icon darkens, release the mouse button. (As an alternative, you could open the floppy-disk window and drag the files you want to copy into the window.)
- The Macintosh operating system will present an animation telling you that it is copying the files.
- If there is not enough room on the floppy disk to hold all the files that you have selected, the operating system will tell you so. If that happens, select fewer files and try again.
- To eject a floppy disk from your floppy drive, do the following:
    □ Select the floppy-disk icon by clicking on it once. The icon will darken.
    □ Wait a moment.
    □ With the cursor pointed at the floppy-disk icon, depress and hold down the mouse button, and drag the floppy-disk icon to the trash can.
    □ The floppy disk will come out of the floppy drive.

---

[4]If you have one of the newer Macs that does not have a floppy-disk drive, you will need to find another means of transporting files. Probably the easiest way is to send the files as enclosures with one or more email messages. If you need to send a lot of large files, you will probably want to use a program such as DropStuff or StuffIt to compress the files into an archive and then send the archive as an email enclosure.

Copying Files from a Floppy Disk to a Hard Disk

Instructions for Windows Users

This procedure is basically the mirror image of the procedure for copying files from your hard disk to a floppy disk.

- Place the floppy disk containing the files that you want to copy in your floppy-disk drive.
- Open My Computer by left double-clicking the icon with that name on your Windows desktop.
- Open the 3 1/2 Floppy [A:] window by left double-clicking on its icon.
- Open the folder on your hard disk into which you want to copy the files that are currently on the floppy disk.
- Arrange the 3 1/2 Floppy [A:] window and the window into which you want to copy the files so that the names of the files you want to copy are visible. If your desktop is crowded, only a small part of the window into which you want to copy the files needs to be visible.
- Use your left mouse button to select one or more files. You know when you have selected a file because it darkens.
- Point the cursor at the darkened area, hold down the left mouse button, and drag the files into the destination folder window
- Windows will present an animation telling you that it is copying the files.
- When the copying process is completed, remove the floppy disk from the floppy drive by pressing the button on the front of the drive.

Instructions for Macintosh Users

This procedure is basically the mirror image of the procedure for copying files from your hard disk to a floppy disk.

- Place the floppy disk containing the files that you want to copy in your floppy-disk drive.
- The floppy disk icon will appear on the right-hand side of your desktop in the first available space under the icon for your startup disk.
- Open the folder into which you want to copy the files.
- Open the floppy disk window.
- Arrange the floppy-disk window and the window into which you want to copy the files so that the names of the files you want to copy

are visible. If your desktop is crowded, only a small part of the window into which you want to copy the files needs to be visible.

- Use your mouse button to select the files that you want to copy. You know when you have selected a file because it darkens.
- Point the cursor at the darkened area, hold down the mouse button, drag the files into the destination window, and release the mouse button.
- The Macintosh operating system will present an animation telling you that it is copying the files.
- To eject a floppy disk from your floppy drive, do the following:
  - ☐ Select the floppy-disk icon by clicking on it once. The icon will darken.
  - ☐ Wait a moment.
  - ☐ With the cursor pointed at the floppy-disk icon, depress and hold down the mouse button, and drag the floppy-disk icon to the trash can.
  - ☐ The floppy disk will come out of the floppy drive.

Using Sniffy Lite for Macintosh Files on a Windows PC and Vice Versa

Sniffy Lite files that were produced on a Macintosh are fully compatible with Sniffy Lite Windows files and vice versa. You can create a file on one kind of computer and look at the file on the other kind of computer. You can even set up an experiment on one kind of computer, save the file when the experiment is in progress, and then complete the experiment on the other kind of computer.

To transfer files from a Windows PC to a Macintosh:

- Copy the Sniffy Lite for Windows files onto a floppy disk.
- Insert the floppy disk into a Macintosh. (If your Macintosh is capable of reading and writing 1.4 MB floppy disks and of running Sniffy, then you should be able to read from or write to a PC floppy provided that the proper Apple software is installed.)
- When you open the floppy-disk window, you will notice that all the Sniffy Lite for Windows file names end with the .sdf suffix. This will be true even though the suffix is ordinarily invisible in Windows.
- Copy the Sniffy Lite for Windows files onto your Macintosh hard disk.
- Start your Sniffy Lite for the Macintosh program.

- Use the Open command on the File menu to open the Sniffy Lite for Windows files.
- If you plan to use the files in Windows again, be sure to save each file with the .sdf suffix appended to each file name.

To transfer files from a Macintosh to a Windows PC:

- Save the files that you want to transfer on the Macintosh hard disk with the .sdf suffix appended to each file name. The Windows version of Sniffy Lite needs the suffix to recognize the files as Sniffy files.
- Be sure that the floppy disk onto which you are going to copy your Macintosh files has been formatted for use on a PC. You can tell whether a floppy disk has been formatted for a PC by looking at the floppy-disk icon on your Macintosh desktop. If necessary, close the floppy-disk window before looking at the icon. The letters "PC" should appear on the closed floppy-disk icon. If the PC identifier is not there, you need to reformat the floppy. To format a floppy for use on a PC, follow these steps:

 Warning: *Reformatting a disk permanently erases any files stored on the disk. Thus you should open the floppy disk window, look at the contents, and move any files that you need to keep somewhere else before you reformat the floppy.*

- ☐ Select the floppy disk by clicking once on its icon.
- ☐ Select the Erase Disk command from the Special menu.
- ☐ In the dialogue box that appears, select DOS 1.4 MB from the drop-down menu that appears to the right of the word "Format."
- ☐ Click on the Erase command button at the bottom of the dialogue box.
- Copy the Sniffy Lite for Macintosh files onto your PC-formatted floppy disk.
- Copy the files from the floppy disk onto your Windows hard disk.
- Start your Sniffy Lite for Windows program.
- Use the Open command under the File menu to open the Macintosh files.

References

Domjan, M. (1998). *The principles of learning and behavior* (4th ed.). Pacific Grove, CA: Brooks/Cole.

Estes, W. K., & Skinner, B. F. (1941). Some quantitative properties of anxiety. *Journal of Experimental Psychology, 29,* 390–400.

Ferster, C. B., & Skinner, B. F. (1957). *Schedules of reinforcement.* New York: Appleton-Century-Crofts.

Guthrie, E. R. (1960). *The psychology of learning* (rev. ed.). Gloucester, MA: Smith.

Hull, C. L. (1943). *Principles of behavior.* New York: Appleton-Century-Crofts.

Hull, C. L. (1952). *A behavior system.* New Haven, CT: Yale University Press.

James, W. (1890). *Principles of psychology.* New York: Holt.

Keller, F. S. & Schoenfold, W. N. (1950). *Principles of psychology.* New York: Appleton-Century-Crofts.

Kimble, G. A. (1961). *Hilgard & Marquis' conditioning and learning* (2nd ed.) New York: Appleton-Century-Crofts.

Mazur, J. E. (1998). *Learning and behavior* (4th ed.). Upper Saddle River, NJ: Prentice Hall.

Pavlov, I. P. (1927). *Conditioned reflexes* (trans. G. V. Anrep). London: Oxford University Press.

Rescorla, R. A., & Wagner, A. R. (1972). An theory of Pavlovian conditioning: Variations in the effectiveness of reinforcement and nonreinforcement. In A. H. Black & W. F. Prokasy (Eds.), *Classical conditioning II: Current research and theory* (pp. 64–99). New York: Appleton-Century-Crofts.

Reynolds, G. S. (1975). *A primer of operant conditioning.* Glenview, IL: Scott, Foresman.

Schwartz, B., & Reisberg, D. (1991). *Learning and memory.* New York: W. W. Norton.

Skinner, B. F. (1930). On the conditions of elicitation of certain eating reflexes. *Proceedings of the National Academy of Science* (Washington, DC), 433–438.

Skinner, B. F. (1935). Two types of conditioned reflexes and a pseudo type. *Journal of General Psychology, 12,* 66–77.

Skinner, B. F. (1938). *The behavior of organisms.* New York: Appleton-Century-Crofts.

Skinner, B. F. (1953). *Science and human behavior.* New York: Macmillan.

Skinner, B. F. (1971). *Beyond rreedom and dignity.* New York: Alfred A. Knopf.

Tarpy, R. M. (1997). *Contemporary learning theory and research.* New York: McGraw-Hill.

Thorndike, E. L. (1898). Animal intelligence: An experimental study of associative processes in animals. *Psychological Monographs, 2,* No. 8.

Tolman, E. C. (1932). *Purposive behavior in animals and men.* New York: Appleton-Century-Crofts.

Index